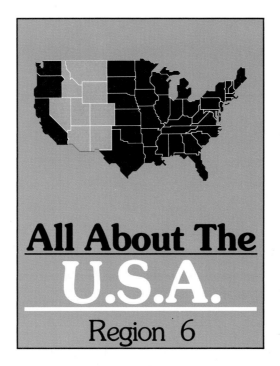

All About The
U.S.A.
Region 6

THE
LOFTY
ONES

by
Allan Carpenter

ENCYCLOPAEDIA BRITANNICA EDUCATIONAL CORPORATION

Indexer and Assistant to the Author
CARL PROVORSE

Copy Preparation
VALERIE ROEBKE

Graphic Designer
ISAAK GRAZUTIS

Typography by
LAW BULLETIN PUBLISHING COMPANY

A Word from the Author — Apologia?

One of the author's favorite characters from Lewis Carroll claimed that he could do anything he pleased with words, and with language in general. Over a period of 45 years in publishing, and after 199 books bearing his name, the author at last claims the right to manipulate the language as it pleases him. If he prefers to save his text at the expense of uneven spacing of the paragraphs, he hopes he may do so. If he wants to use an incomplete sentence or to capitalize a word at some time or use a hyphen sometimes and not do either at other times, or to use a hyphen sometimes and not at others—or to use a dash—he now claims the right to do so, by virtue of age, if not senility. It is not often that an author finds editors who are willing to indulge such whims. The editors at Britannica are not only meticulous but also caring, and they have given this author carte blanche in the production of a work which is based on his 45 years of specialized study of the states. So, if such eccentricities and inconsistencies appear in this work and if blame should fall, the author wishes it to be known that he accepts all blame as well as credit, if any.

ISBN 0-8347-3391-9
Library of Congress Catalog Card Number 86-080849

Opposite, "San Francisco Peaks," by Bertha Menzler Dresser, captures much of the "romance" of the Old West, with its high mountains, sparse vegetation and pioneering travel, courtesy Santa Fe Southern Pacific Corp

Contents

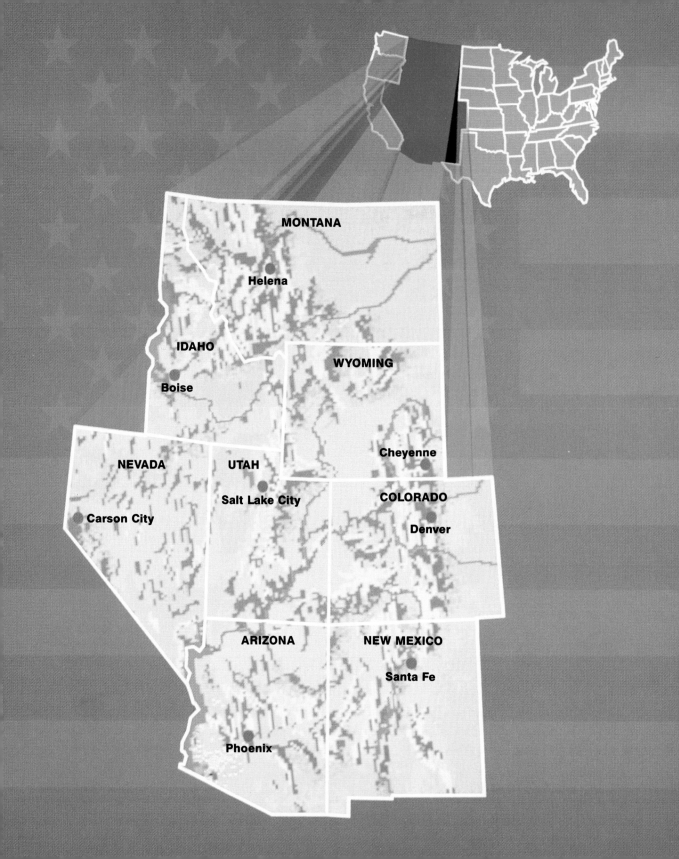

THE LOFTY ONES—OVERVIEW

FASCINATING REGION

"The grandest spectacle in the world" cuts across the region. Someone else has called it, "the most colorful gash anywhere." However, other experts have other favorites for scenic magnificence and beauty, and an incredible number of them can also be found in the region, perhaps more dramatic and varied landscape than exists anywhere else in a similar area.

In its prehistoric times, the region cradled the most advanced and interesting civilization in what is now the United States. Those early dwellers left ghost cities of stone and adobe construction, which are marvels of building skill even by today's standards.

More recent "ghosts" also dot the landscape, cities that mushroomed with the discovery of wealth, and then were abandoned when the wealth faded, becoming poignant reminders of the region's historic past.

No United States presidents were born in the region, but some of the most notable Indian leaders led their followers in ways that ranged from peaceful statesmanship to the longest and most violent struggles between the two races.

The brilliant administrative genius of one of the world's most effective religious leaders laid the foundation for a striking civilization in the wilderness—and for the worldwide outreach of a religious philosophy.

On a lesser scale the region has such interesting sidelights as the miraculous stairway, the lake that roars, the famous thirteenth stairstep, the many curves of the main street of a capital city and the reason they came about, the mystery of the giant moccasins and the mountain view that gave a woman great fame.

Perhaps most interesting is one of the many reminders of the constant possibility of human error—the mountain which a famed explorer said could never be climbed, but which now is scaled by more than 500,000 people every year.

THE SWEEP OF GEOGRAPHY

Nowhere in the country, perhaps nowhere in the world, does the landscape have such varied and majestic sweep. That "purple mountain majesty" was made famous by the song which that majesty itself had inspired.

The backbone of the continent thrusts up from one edge of the region to the other. Even the lowlands are "high," with the region having the greatest average height of all and boasting the nation's two highest state capitals.

The region is renowned for its depth as well as its height, with the deepest canyon and the deepest cave as well as the greatest number of underground rivers.

Four of the mightiest rivers twist to some of their farthest inland points in widespread sections of the region. By contrast, two portions of the area are surrounded on all sides so that their rainfall never reaches any sea or gulf.

Nomadic Indians hunt buffalo on the Great Plains

One of them is the largest of its type in the country.

A number of the country's largest manmade lakes have spread new life-giving water over vast areas. Several of the natural lakes have been ranked by experts as among the most beautiful anywhere. The natural lakes also include one of the strangest and most unusual. At one time, portions of the region were covered with enormous lakes, formed by the melting waters of the glaciers.

The more exotic forces of nature have dealt the region some of the world's most intriguing wonders. They include the greatest clusters of thermal activity anywhere, along with the world's largest mineral hot spring.

Nowhere is there a more peculiar and compelling landscape than that found in many parts of the region that have been covered with lava in an endless array of fanciful shapes.

Some of the finest fossils of prehistoric creatures have been found in the region, including the largest single deposits of dinosaur relics. Other unusual discoveries include the nest of dinosaur eggs and the dental remains discovered in 1985-86, which may be identified as the long-sought missing link to mankind.

THE SWEEP OF HISTORY

One of the major cities of the region takes its name from a legendary bird. Not too far to the north is another major city which was saved from possible early destruction by a more common kind of bird.

Other cities of the area once were bustling centers of perhaps the most advanced civilization developed in the present United States before the coming of Europeans. Certainly that early civilization was even more civilized in some of the ways of peace. In matters of agricultural practices, engineering and many forms of art, that early civilization could also hold its own. This was particularly true in architecture, which provided remarkable homes still in use centuries after they were constructed.

By the time Europeans arrived in numbers, this civilization had dwindled. More numerous were the nomadic and often fierce Indian tribes, some of whom had borrowed various advances from their city-dwelling neighbors.

One of the finest skills was in basket making, developed by some tribes to a point never excelled by others. The traditions of pottery making of the finest and most artistic types and the crafting of splendid jewelry have also been handed down across the centuries. By contrast, other tribes of the region are considered to have been among the most primitive on the continent.

One of the earliest of all the great explorations covered a wide sweep of the area. The adventurers learned much about the regions they passed through but failed to find the riches they were looking for, although actually there were more riches in the region than anyone at the time could even have dreamed of finding.

One of the earliest attempts at settlement was also one of the most interesting and picturesque, involving beautiful Spanish ladies in colorful gowns, dashingly dressed Spanish caballeros and flocks of animals which stunned the Indians by their number.

One of the greatest explorations of all

time did much to learn new facts about the region, including substantial reports on the native peoples, scientific facts about the plants and animals, and, of course, much new information about the geography of the region.

The vast unknown reaches of mountain and plain still called on all the resources of some of the most skilled pathfinders and scouts, including a woman scout who may have surpassed them all.

The newly explored routes were soon put to use in a volume of traffic that no one would have thought possible. All the major trails crossed the region, bringing thousands of religious refugees followed by others whose religion was the search for gold and other mineral wealth.

That mineral wealth brought the almost instant creation of mining towns and cities. Their unique blend of saloon and opera house produced flourishing communities, some of which flourish even today and others of which vanished, leaving only their building shells as traces.

As settlement advanced, conflicts spread among the newcomers and the Indians, between the cattle growers and the farmers and between the cattlemen and the sheepmen. Indian wars involved some of the most aggressive tribes as well as some of those most opposed to warfare. Decades of war climaxed in the most famous loss of government troops at the hands of Indian forces.

Before effective formal governments were formed at various times and places in the region, peaceful citizens were also harrassed by some of the country's worst outlaw leaders and bands of thieves and cutthroats, including perhaps the most

"Indians Attacking Overland Train," by Charles Craig

notorious of all the lawbreakers.

The Equality State lived up to its slogan by bringing to the fore one of the chief advocates of women's rights, by giving women the right to vote—even before statehood—and by electing one of the first two women governors and the first woman elected to the U.S. House of Representatives. Other states of the region also have long had concerns about equal rights and opportunities.

Recent times have brought vast expansion of population, especially in the southwest, along with great increases in population of many of the major cities.

PERSONALITY PLUS

One of the Indian groups was called "the noblest of them all." One of their leaders was also noted for his nobility of spirit, loyalty, administrative ability and military judgment. Others provided some of the most warlike leadership to match their great military talents, which they pitted for so long against the hated newcomers. One of the Indian leaders of the region was a notable diplomat and statesman.

The most noted of all scouts, frontiersmen and traders plied their various trades in the wilderness. Some became known around the world, and towns were named for them.

Others of America's best-known figures acquired their wealth in rooting out minerals or in consolidating the mining properties first worked by others. Some of these tycoons lost all they had and died in poverty, while others went on to

8

establish American family dynasties.

The region has been rich in artistic and literary tradition since the earliest days. Pioneer artists of the Old West gained international reputations painting and sculpting the western scenes they knew best, and that tradition is being carried on by modern artists, including many famed potters and weavers.

One of the most unusual artists never learned to read or write, spent most of her time living outdoors, has never been generally acknowledged for her work but is considered by many to have been one of the world's truly great artists.

One of America's foremost writers first gained fame as a reporter for a pioneer western newspaper, which in itself was admired as an artistic achievement. One of the country's most famed modern authors spent his last days in a small Idaho community.

Among American leaders who deserve much higher regard for their accomplishments than they usually receive, one in this region was known for developing his religious philosophy and as an administrator and political leader of the highest order.

A CONCENTRATION OF WEALTH

The region is well supplied with fossil fuels, including great reserves of coal. However, it is better known for being the nation's premiere supplier of silver as well as one of the leaders in gold, zinc and lead. Several states lay claim to "the richest hill on earth." One of them may well have saved the Union during the Civil War.

Although the present outlook for copper is depressed, the region remains the principal source of the nation's copper supplies.

PEOPLES

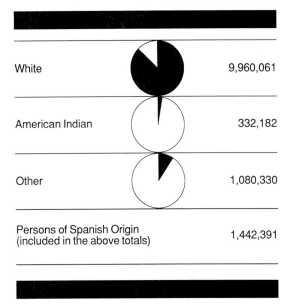

White	9,960,061
American Indian	332,182
Other	1,080,330
Persons of Spanish Origin (included in the above totals)	1,442,391

The region leads in some of the more unusual minerals, including molybdenum, turquoise, phosphate and opals. The world's largest black opal came from the region, which is a heaven on earth for gem and rock hounds, with almost every semiprecious mineral known, scattered about the region in profusion.

The vast herds of buffalo and endless prairie dog towns have disappeared, but the region supports a surprising number of wild creatures both great and small. One of them has an unusual reputation as a thief. One of the state birds is particularly noted for its unusual habits.

Each state of the region has supplies of timber which, taken together, offer enough wood for the nation's use over a long period. No one state is using more timber than it returns to production.

Flora of the region ranges from the gaunt giants of the desert, with arms

THE ECONOMY

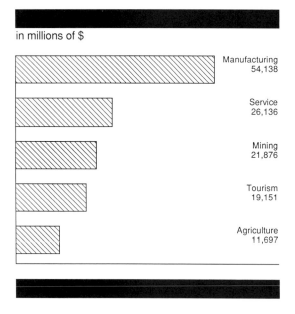

in millions of $

Manufacturing	54,138
Service	26,136
Mining	21,876
Tourism	19,151
Agriculture	11,697

raised like coatracks or organ pipes, to the tiny wildflowers of the alpine valleys, from the ephemeral prairie grasses to the world's oldest living things.

The region has experienced a number of notable records in transportation and communication. With an interesting ceremony, the first great transcontinental railroad was joined in the heart of the region. Perhaps the most interesting part of its dedication was the great embarrassment of the governor who presided.

To the far south the region boasts of the oldest road in the nation, the much-discussed short life of the Pony Express, and—far inland though it is—the region now has access to each ocean.

Wheat to the north and cotton to the south are the major crops, but livestock still brings in the greatest agricultural income to the area.

TRAVELERS' CHOICE

When asked what place in the United States they would like to see, world travelers would probably rank high two destinations in the region—one for its two G's, gambling and glamor; the other for its scenic magnificence.

Even the most hardened travelers stand in awe at the rim of the Grand Canyon. The gambling, the nightclubs, the "glamor" have made the once tiny desert town of Las Vegas one of the most glittering and alluring travel attractions in the world.

However, the region has an incredible number of other attractions, many of them unique in the world. Many have not received anything like the attention they deserve, and it is likely that some still remain to be discovered. Actually, a number of areas in the region have never been fully explored.

President Theodore Roosevelt walked all day across the desert to see Utah's Rainbow Bridge. This global traveler called it "one of the wonders of the world." Hundreds of these arches make the region unique. In addition, southern Utah alone offers several national sites, each renowned for its special attractions. The lofty spires of Monument Valley have no counterpart.

The lakes of the region present a range of attractions, from the high, cool beauty of Coeur d'Alene, Tahoe and other mountain beauties through the eerie solitude of Great Salt Lake, to the desert lands transformed by Lake Mead and Lake Powell.

The individual natural wonders are numberless. Nothing can duplicate the attractions of Carlsbad Cavern and its

Many of the tribal activities may still be observed. "Buffalo Dance at Mishongnovi," by Louis H. Sharp

cloud of bats. Devil's Tower literally stands alone. Teton National Park, Glacier National Park, the Craters of the Moon, Pikes Peak and some of the world's most scenic highways are only a few of the better known.

Nowhere else can a traveler experience the thrill of investigating the culture of the extraordinary Pueblo people. Taos Pueblo has kept much of the old life alive, and visitors can experience the thrill of the past. Not to be outdone, modern society has also provided ghost towns across the region. A visit to a selected number of them could fill a whole vacation.

Far from being ghost towns, the major cities of the region provide attractions all their own. Denver and Phoenix can hardly keep up with the population growth and the host of new and interesting shops and restaurants. Salt Lake City is quite unlike any other.

But the cities are not neglecting their past. Albuquerque has restored its Old Town, and Denver has recreated many of its historic districts. Santa Fe is determined to keep its historic charm, centered around its quaint square.

But Santa Fe also has kept up-to-date with one of the world's leading presentations of opera, heard in a wonderful pavilion under the stars. The art galleries and shops of Santa Fe can hardly be equalled anywhere and seem incredible for such a small community.

However, other small communities of the region have a surprising variety of activities. The university town of Moscow, Idaho, along with neighboring Pull-

"Life on the Prairie — The Last of the Buffalo Hunters"

man, Washington, boasts a symphony and ballet of very substantial merit. Other university cities of the region, particularly Tucson, with its great museums, provide a wide variety of attractions.

Most of the communities have their particular annual events, but America's oldest festival, Fiesta de Santa Fe, and Frontier Days at Cheyenne, with "the world's best rodeo," rank among the country's most notable annual celebrations.

Many other fine rodeos, Custer battlefield, Hoover Dam, the world's highest bridge, the Air Force Academy, Dinosaur Land—the variety and interest of the attractions go on and on.

For some visitors—among them, famed author Ernie Pyle—an "invisible" attraction is the best of all. When Pyle sprawled out, arms and legs widespread on a bare patch of ground, he was doing something that can be done nowhere else. He was lying in four states at once at the only point in the U.S. where four state corners come together.

Indeed, this is a region where many of the attractions of the world have come together.

ARIZONA

FASCINATING ARIZONA

Within the borders of Arizona lies the "grandest spectacle on earth," the sight more people want to see than any other on the continent.

However, this great attraction is almost matched by many others in the state, which is growing so fast it doesn't quite know what to do.

Of course, not everything about Arizona is grand and spectacular. The state has its many more modest but interesting touches.

Few states can provide so many interesting sidelights of nature, such as the river that stayed and the banks that rose, the river with the world's fastest navigable rapids and the big stone mittens of the desert.

Arizona is the state where travelers have been saved by the water pitchers of the desert, where people sometimes "take the rap" for a thieving rat, where some of the great plants have accordian pleats, and where the pipe organs of the desert only accompany choirs of birds.

The sweep of great historical events covers hundreds of years, but within the accounts of the great events are scores of smaller accounts of human interest, such as the prehistoric construction of the first skyscraper.

The history of Arizona tells of a great city that was named for a legendary bird, of another city named for a flagpole. Arizona history recounts how the devil came in breathing fire from his nose and kicking water with his feet; it is the state where much of the longest war in history was fought; where a burro discovered gold; and where lost gold mines have never been found, but the search for them is fun.

Starting in Arizona, visitors can visit three other states in a matter of seconds; they can marvel at the dome of the beautiful mission which was completed by Indians searching for coins. At that same mission, legend says that a cat and mouse may cause the end of the world.

However, that fate causes little fear among the thousands of new citizens who flock in to make Arizona one of the fastest-growing states, or for the millions of visitors who are determined that they must see all the wonders of the Grand Canyon State.

THE FACE OF ARIZONA

Looking down on the Grand Canyon from the air, a traveler would see "The most sublime spectacle on earth," as explorer John Wesley Powell described it. From below, a hiker looks upward for a mile and sees layer after layer, color after brilliant color, of rocks and earth.

Those two perspectives illustrate some of the wonders and infinite variety of the canyon, which is not only perhaps the most awesome and beautiful sight anywhere but also one of the most revealing about the story of the earth.

Every layer, every color of soil, tells the geologist a great deal about the planet's past—a great natural picture book stretching almost back to the earth's beginnings.

As the earth slowly rose, the Colorado River carved into the rocks. Wind carrying sand and rain, freezing and thawing, added to the carving process

THAT'S CURIOUS:

The Colorado River is not much deeper in the earth than it was millions of years ago. As the land slowly rose, the river cut into it and stayed almost the same level. Actually, the rim has risen about a mile.

until the forces together had eaten away to a width of 4 to 14 miles, and had gouged down a depth of more than a mile, along more than 200 miles of the river bed.

The walls of the canyon also reveal the skeletons of creatures that lived at the time the various layers were formed, from primitive algae near the bottom to higher forms of life near the top.

Vast as the canyon is, it covers only a small percentage of the sixth largest state where there are other natural wonders almost as magnificent, including wonderful Oak Creek Canyon; its colors are perhaps even deeper than those of the Grand Canyon.

Arizona slopes upward through three major regions, from the lowest point on the southwest to the high plateau country of the northeast.

Thirty different mountain chains punctuate the land. They include the mysterious Chiracauas, the White Mountains and the Santa Catalinas. Some of the mountains rise dramatically out of the plains region.

The Colorado River drains most of the state as it enters the northern boundary, hurries westward, then takes a dramatic curve to flow almost directly southward. The Little Colorado, Gila River and the Bill Williams River carry additional water across a thirsty land.

The entire border with California is formed by the Colorado River, along with more than half the border with Nevada.

Opposite, Phoenix

A glance at the map will show that a small part of the Colorado River border separates Arizona and Mexico. The other borders are manmade, with Utah to the north, New Mexico on the east and Mexico itself on the south.

Arizona has its own 90 degree share of the only place in the country where four states come together, a point on the map known as the Four Corners.

In this naturally dry land, all the major lakes are artificial. Lake Mead, shared with Nevada, is the best known. Glen Canyon Dam is in Arizona, but most of Lake Powell behind the dam is in Utah. Below Hoover Dam, several smaller dams and lakes block the free flow of the Colorado River as it enters Mexico on its way to the Gulf of California. A number of smaller reservoirs have been formed by dams in the Arizona interior.

Eons ago, this dry land was covered by water as the oceans moved in a number of times.

Few other places can boast of as many striking formations of rocks and mountain crags and desert wonders, twisted valleys and other evidence of the titanic forces of nature. They include the power of volcanoes such as Sunset Crater, built up only about 1000 years ago.

The hot, dry climate which kept explorers and settlers away for centuries has become the state's greatest attraction as a place where winter can generally be abandoned for warm, clear air.

15

EARLY DWELLERS

Very early peoples in Arizona have been named Cochise Man. They probably hunted mastodons and grew crops, as shown by their traces at Sulphur Spring Valley. A group called Basketmakers occupied cave homes at one time but went on to live in pit houses. Even later, they built houses of stone and masonry above ground.

Perhaps the Basketmakers developed further to become the group we know as Pueblo people. Or perhaps other more advanced groups came in and drove the Basketmakers out. The Pueblo continued to prosper and build even larger homes and communities.

For protection many of the early dwellers built large communities in deep natural recesses high up on the cliffs. They are known as Cliffdwellers. The cliff dwelling known as Montezuma Castle was reached by a series of ladders and rises for five stories within its niche of the cliff.

Because of the quality of their adobe brick construction and the very dry air of Arizona, the relics of this surprising Pueblo civilization have survived in several parts of the state. They left behind handsome jewelry of turquoise, clay figures and pottery and handsome woven items.

During the Pueblo period, desert people also developed a civilization known as Hohokam, or "ancient ones" in the Pima Indian language. These Canal Builders engineered extensive irrigation systems, some of which are restored and used even today. Built 800 years ago, perhaps with the help of Pueblo masons, the Hohokam town now called Casa

Grande had a structure described today as the first skyscraper.

As Europeans first came in, probably only one group of Indians could be called descendants of the Pueblo—the Hopi. They were part of the larger group known as Uto-Aztecan. Others of this group were the Papago, Pima and Kaibab Paiute. The other major groups are called the Athapascan and Yuman.

The Hopi remain today much as they were in earlier times, making fine baskets, enjoying their ceremonials and other traditions. They were led by a woman, and property was transferred from the mother.

The Pima and Papago were the most friendly to the Europeans, treating them, as one explorer wrote, "immeasurably before them [Europeans] in honesty and virtue."

The Athapascan were the largest group found by the early explorers. They were the Apache and Navajo, who arrived not much earlier than the first explorers. The Navajo increased their strength by stealing horses and attacking the Pueblo tribes and early Spanish people.

The fierce Apache had many beliefs about nature and religion. Each of their tribal groups had a male war chief, and a female chief was the principal ruler.

The small Yuman family group was made up of the warlike Mojave, the Hualpai and the Havasupai. The latter still live at the bottom of the Grand Canyon, where they were first found.

STIRRINGS

In 1539 Friar Marcos de Niza was the first explorer known to have visited present Arizona. He was accompanied by Estevan, a former black slave. Estevan was executed by the Zuni Indians. Father de Niza returned to Mexico, telling tales of the rich cities in the north.

One of the great explorations of all time was mounted by Francisco de Coronado, guided by Father de Niza. Cardenas, one of Coronado's assistants, found the Grand Canyon, later described as a horrid canyon which kept people from the life-giving waters of the river.

Hernando de Alarcon found the mouth of the Colorado River and poled his way northward by boat into present Arizona. Other expeditions came and went in the area with little success.

Missionary work among the Hopi Indians began in the early 1600's. They were driven out in 1680. Jesuit priests came in 1692. Jesuit Father Eusebio Francisco Kino established 24 missions, including seven in present Arizona.

The first fort, Tubac, was not established until 1752, first permanent European settlement in present Arizona.

Tucson was established in 1775.

When the Spanish king banished the Jesuits in 1776, Franciscan Padre Francisco Tomas Garces carried on the work, built the famous San Xavier del Bac, or White Dove Mission, and carried Christianity as far as the Colorado River.

Father Garces was killed by Indians in 1781, and during the Mexican revolution the region was in turmoil for several decades. Only Tubac and Tucson remained in what is now Arizona.

During the American War with Mexico, the expeditionary forces of Colonel Stephen W. Kearny and the Mormon Battalion struggled through Arizona on

"Street Scene, Hopi Pueblo," by Louis Akin

their way to the war in California and blazed a trail to the coast.

EARLY GROWTH

The army trail was followed by thousands on their way to the California gold fields; many of them decided not to go on and settled in Arizona. The region became a part of the Territory of New Mexico in 1850. Yuma became a shipping point on the Colorado River. When gold was discovered, Gila City mushroomed; then, with the failure of the gold, it became a ghost city.

In 1861 the scattered residents of Arizona voted to join the Confederacy, and Confederate cavalry arrived in Tucson in 1862. They soon were driven out by Union forces. Arizona Territory was created in 1863.

Phoenix had a small start in 1866. When Jack Swilling discovered the ancient canals there, he formed a company to restore some of them and within a year irrigated crops were growing, and a small community sprang up.

The Indian wars of the plains are said to be the lengthiest of any in world history. The fierce Indians could retreat into their mountain hideaways and never be found. Apache Chief Cochise was never captured. The Navajo finally were subdued by frontiersman Colonel Kit Carson, and 8,000 were led into captivity.

Seeking vengeance for his wife and children, Apache Chief Geronimo was one of the last of the Indian foes. He finally surrendered and died at Fort Sill, Oklahoma, in 1909.

For peaceful early settlers, outlaws were almost as troublesome as the Indians. However, as the population grew, troubles lessened. Population advanced as many former Confederates came in from the southern states. In the 1870's and 80's Mormon settlements were founded, including Fredonia and Littlefield.

UP-TO-DATE

Prescott and Tucson alternated as territorial capital until 1889, when Phoenix was chosen permanently.

In 1911, when the Salt River was dammed to make Theodore Roosevelt Lake, it was the first national reclamation project and greatly hastened the state's growth. Statehood came in 1912.

Grand Canyon became a national park in 1913.

Troubles with Mexico plagued the border. Then the larger conflict of World War I called thousands from Arizona.

In 1929 the Navajo Bridge across Marble Canyon became the first direct highway link with Utah. The 1934 "water war" was "fought" with California over California's plan to use Colorado River water. Arizona lost through a Supreme Court decision.

The year 1937 was notable for the first one-man float trip down the Colorado, by Buzz Hostrom. It was not until 1938 that the first women boated the Colorado.

The recent history of Arizona has been dominated by its fantastic popularity and growth in both population and commerce. Aided by air conditioning for the hot days, new jobs and vast irrigation for crops, hydroelectric power and attractions for retired persons, "sunbeltomania" descended on the state.

In the 14 years from 1970 through 1984, the state's population almost doubled. In just 12 years, from 1970, Phoenix added over 100,000 people, and Tucson skyrocketed from 50,000 in 1950 to 350,000 in 1982.

The presidential elections of 1980 and 1984 in Arizona were won handily by Ronald Reagan. But Governor Bruce E. Babbitt retained the Democratic hold on the statehouse.

PERSONALITIES

Barry Morris Goldwater was born in Phoenix. He began his career in the family department store. World War II called him into service. He held only minor public offices until he was elected to the Senate in 1953. He was known for his stand against Communism and big government.

In 1964 Goldwater gained the Republican presidential nomination. His opponent, Lyndon Johnson, was almost exactly Goldwater's opposite in his political ideas. Goldwater lost the election, but he

PEOPLES

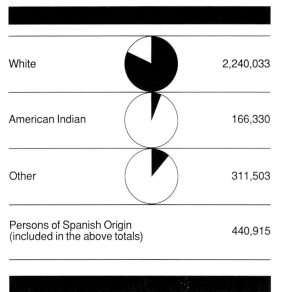

White	2,240,033
American Indian	166,330
Other	311,503
Persons of Spanish Origin (included in the above totals)	440,915

was returned to the Senate in 1968.

Whether or not his party held the Senate majority, Goldwater has remained one of the most powerful figures in Washington.

By contrast, one of Arizona's earliest leaders devoted his life to religion and exploration. During the years 1692 to 1711, Father Eusebio Francisco Kino preached and taught in Arizona and Mexico. In spite of hardships from the desert heat and often hostile Indians, Father Kino established missions, taught the Indians new methods of agriculture and baptized thousands into Christianity.

As an explorer, Father Kino pushed as far north as the Colorado River and established a crude road across the southwestern part of present Arizona.

Another churchman, Father Francisco Tomas Garces, also reached the Colorado River, but he did more, becoming one of the first Europeans to descend to the bottom. He gave the river its name, meaning "colored red" because of the red silt it carried. He visited the Havasupai Indians at the bottom of the canyon.

Father Garces helped to blaze a more permanent trail to the Colorado River, which became part of the route to the Spanish missions on the Pacific coast.

John Wesley Powell came to Arizona in 1869 to make a geological survey of the Colorado River for the Smithsonian Institution. Despite the loss of an arm during the battle of Shiloh, in 1869 Powell led the first exploratory trip down the Colorado, taming its rapids for the first time.

Although he is best known for that feat, Powell made significant contributions to the knowledge of geology and peoples of the area.

His efforts were mainly responsible for the creation of the U.S. Geological Survey, and he served as its director. He also was the director of the Bureau of American Ethnology. His books and reports provided much of the early knowledge of the southwest.

After being shipwrecked in the Gulf of California, Charles D. Poston and Herman Ehrenberg crossed into present Arizona and began silver mining operations at Tubac. Poston was given much credit for persuading Congress to give Arizona territorial status. He served as the territorial delegate to Congress and has frequently been called the Father of Arizona.

The hard life of the Arizona frontier produced many notable pioneers. Pete Kitchen "...was the only settler whom the Apache could not dislodge. They made raid after raid, and shot his pigs...killed his bravest neighbors...and slaughtered his stepson, but Pete Kitchen fought on undaunted. His name struck terror to every Apache heart."

A town, river and mountain in Arizona are named for Bill Williams, who lived for ten years with the Osage Indians. "Indian signs were an open book to him, and he was even readier to take a scalp than an Apache."

Al Sieber became known as the Man of Iron because of his stern work as a government scout in controlling the fierce Apache. In later life he suffered hard times, with no help from the government he had worked to preserve. As a construction worker on the Roosevelt Dam, Sieber was killed saving the life of an Apache workman on his crew.

A much better-known name on the frontier was that of Wyatt Earp, who served as deputy U.S. marshall at Tombstone. His name was linked to many stories of bravery and cunning, but he was not very respected by the local people. His life has been glamorized in later years by movies and television.

Among creative Arizonans, Oliver La Farge was awarded the Pulitzer Prize for his novel "Laughing Boy."

Arizona humorist Dick Wick Hall gained national fame with his stories of Arizona.

THAT'S CURIOUS:

Typical of Dick Wick Hall's humor was his tall tale that "...we sometimes have to plant onions in between the rows of potatoes and then scratch the onions to make the potatoes' eyes water enough to irrigate the rest of the garden."

A renowned painting of the canyon is "The Chasm of the Colorado," by Thomas Moran, which hangs in the capitol at Washington.

A dramatic musical description of America's greatest natural wonder is found in Ferde Grofe's "Grand Canyon Suite."

A WEALTH OF NATURE

The dry climate of Arizona has produced many unusual plants. Cacti often grow where nothing else can survive. Cacti have developed unique ways of storing the scant rainfall of the desert. A good many desert travelers have been saved by the water stored in the barrel cactus, which can store the most liquid of all.

In spring the desert blooms with a very beautiful display if the rainfall is adequate. The waxy bloom of the giant saguaro cactus was chosen as the state flower. The pleated walls of the great saguaro plant expand in times of rainfall and contract as they use the stored moisture to keep alive. Some can live for five years without rainfall.

The saguaro is so much admired that "cactus-nappers" operate undercover to steal the protected plants from the desert and sell them for a good sum. Efforts are increasing to protect the giant cacti in their natural habitat.

The rare organ cactus, the century plant, the sotol, yucca and Joshua tree, a relative of the yucca, are other interesting desert plants.

A surprising variety of other plants is found across the dry lands and in the highlands.

Many Arizona animals are on the list of hunters, including the popular javelina or wild pig, rare mountain lion, bighorn sheep, turkey, elk and mule deer.

A fascinating little creature is the pack rat. Pack rats will steal almost anything. They have even made off with sticks of dynamite. Three mining partners almost came to blows about thefts in their camp until they discovered that the pack rats were the thieves making off with their valuables.

At the higher altitudes, Arizona's forests include stands of pine, spruce, aspen, junipers, Arizona cypress and pinon pine.

The gila monster is the only poisonous lizard in the country. The gentle horned toad became such a popular pet that it was threatened with extinction in the wild. Tarantulas are also becoming popular pets; they reach a size six inches across, and their bite is not very dangerous.

The Kaibab squirrel, found only on the north rim of the Grand Canyon, the thick-billed parrots of the Chiricahua Mountains and the Arizona native trout, found nowhere else, are other unusual creatures.

Copper, gold, silver and a wide variety of other minerals, as well as gemstones and petrified wood are valuable resources.

Water is the most prized mineral of all. With the rapidly sinking water table, experts worry that the state may not keep up with the water demands of continuing population growth and expanding agriculture.

USING THE WEALTH

Arizona produces several times more copper than all the other copper-produc-

THE ECONOMY

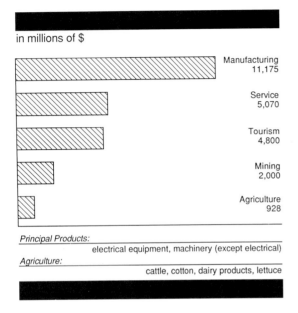

in millions of $

Manufacturing	11,175
Service	5,070
Tourism	4,800
Mining	2,000
Agriculture	928

Principal Products:
electrical equipment, machinery (except electrical)

Agriculture:
cattle, cotton, dairy products, lettuce

ing states combined. Gold and silver and other metals continue to be important.

The discovery of precious minerals brought new communities almost overnight, and then, as the resources dwindled, many Arizona communities became ghost towns. Each one could tell a story of triumph and tragedy.

The legends of lost gold mines have brought gold seekers into the state almost since the beginning of its history. The most famous was the Dutchman mine; Jacob Wolz was said to have killed eight men to keep the mine secret. He was so successful that when he died, the location was lost and never recovered.

Almost 80 percent of Arizona consists of Indian reservations or public lands. Where water is available for irrigation, the soil and climate combine to produce extraordinary crops.

Cotton is the leading agricultural crop. However, the livestock industry has exceeded crops in total income.

The flight of business and industry from the north and east has brought large numbers of new businesses and industry to Arizona, including such giants as Greyhound and its 207 subsidiaries, at their Phoenix headquarters.

The growth is expected to continue until the region stretching from Nogales through Tucson and Phoenix and perhaps even to Las Vegas, Nevada, may become almost united as one great megalopolis. This can only come about, however, if water and other essential resources can be provided in regions where they are so scarce.

Transportation in Arizona has progressed from foot travel through pack animals (even including camels), river steamers and twenty-mule teams, until today all modern systems are available, including some of the most progressive airports.

With the coming of the first steamboat up the Colorado River, the Indians screamed that "the devil was coming blowing fire from his nose and kicking up the water with his feet."

THAT'S CURIOUS:

Arizona's top gold discovery was made by a burro. Henry Wickenburg became so angry at his burro that he threw heavy rocks at the creature. Looking at the rocks more closely, he decided they should be analyzed. The analysis proved the rocks contained gold, and he started the Vulture Mine.

The first railroad tracks crossed the state in 1881.

GETTING AROUND

Arizona license plates carry the slogan "Grand Canyon State," and few would argue that the vast colorful slash in the earth is one of the outstanding wonders of the world, the very essence of grandeur. Standing on the rim, most visitors feel a sense of awe and wonder they have never experienced before. From some vantage points, such as Hopi Point on the south rim, the tiny squiggle of the Colorado River can be seen and sometimes even heard faintly.

This "tiny" stream becomes a roaring, churning torrent when viewed from the bottom of the canyon. Until 1949 only about 100 people had run the rapids; now hundreds brave the torrent every day, totalling about 14,000 breathless navigators every year. The voyage is called "the most dramatic white river trip in the world." It includes Lava Falls, said to be the fastest navigable rapids in the world.

Many visitors ride to the bottom of the canyon on the famous burros. Some hike the long, exciting trails to the bottom. Even experienced hikers find the climbing difficult. Many hikers collapse and have to be dragged out of the canyon.

Every hour, almost every minute, from every spot along both the north and south rims, the view changes, with the

The Grand Canyon

riot of colors, the strange rock formations and the eerie vastness all combining to make this the spectacle of spectacles—the spot most Americans hope to see sometime during their lifetime.

Flagstaff is the nearest large city to the canyon. The city grew around an actual flagstaff erected to celebrate the national centennial in 1876. The All-Indian Pow Wow at Flagstaff is one of the major national festivals.

The handsome cinder cone of Sunset Crater, Wupatki National Monument, Meteor Crater and Walnut Canyon, with its cliff dwellings, are all attractions.

THAT'S CURIOUS:

Edward F. Beale decided that for desert transport, desert animals should be used, so he imported camels. The great beasts could carry heavy loads and proved useful for a time. Some were abandoned or ran away, and they could occasionally be seen plodding over the sand, but they did not survive.

"Navajo Silversmith," by E. Martin Hennings

Northeast Arizona offers another spectacular natural wonder, Monument Valley, with its strange formations, including a lofty pair which look like left and right mittens, and so are called The Mittens.

Farthest northeast is Four Corners, where a visitor may lie stretched across four states. Some visitors run from one to another and claim they have visited four states in only a few seconds.

The Navajo and Hopi reservations occupy much of the northeast, and Canyon de Chelly National Monument is another attraction.

Hoover Dam and Lake Mead bring many visitors to the northwest corner.

South of Flagstaff, the road through Oak Creek Canyon is one of the most dramatic anywhere, especially when the glowing pink and red bluffs reflect the setting sun. At the canyon's end the town of Sedona is an interesting stopping place.

The university city of Tucson anchors southern Arizona. It grew on the site of the prehistoric village called Stjukson from which it took its name. The museums of the University of Arizona are particularly outstanding, including the Arizona State Museum.

The Arizona-Sonora Desert Museum and Saguaro National Monument feature the desert plants, and the museum shows the native animals in their natural habitat.

South of Tucson lies the striking snow white Mission San Xavier del Bac, known as the White Dove of the Desert. Begun in 1768, it is still serving members of the San Xavier Indian Reservation.

Coronado National Memorial and Organ Pipe Cactus National Monument are attractions at the southern border.

Phoenix has become one of the fastest-growing cities in the country. Businesses, retired people and others wanting the cloudless skies and warm sun have swarmed in.

The capitol was completed in 1900, but wings were added, and other buildings now combine to form an imposing capitol complex. The liberty torch and wreath of peace are held aloft by the winged statue at the top of the capitol dome.

Arizona State Museum, Phoenix Art Museum and the Heard Museum of Anthropology and Primitive Arts add greatly to the metropolitan cultural attractions of Phoenix. The Heard Museum is particularly recommended as one of the best in its field.

Among the structures of Arizona State University at Tempe, Frank Lloyd

Wright's Grady Gammage Memorial Auditorium has excited world comment. It has structural and design features that are said to be unique anywhere.

Each year, the Don's Club of Phoenix holds its Superstition Mountain Lost Gold Trek at Lost Dutchman State Park, pretending to search for the almost-legendary lost gold mine.

Desert Botanical Garden at Papago Park displays one of the finest collections of desert plants.

Pueblo Grande Museum preserves some of the best examples of the work of the Hohokam or desert farmers. The museum is operated by the city of Phoenix.

For some visitors this and many other prehistoric ruins are among the most interesting of the many attractions of Arizona.

Largest of these is the complex at Navajo National Monument, preserved on the Navajo tribal lands. This is one of the cultural centers of the Anasazi, or ancient ones, who were Pueblo and not Navajo. Most accessible to visitors is the Betatakin (Ledge) House, deserted about 700 years ago. Built in a natural alcove of the sheer canyon, the ruin has 135 rooms. Keet Seel, the largest individual cliff dwelling in the state, and Inscription House are other ruins of the complex. The latter is too fragile to permit visitors.

Montezuma Castle National Monument preserves two five-story ruins and offers a museum of jewelry, pottery and other artifacts of the Sinagua Indians.

The Museum of Northern Arizona, the Wupatki National Monument, with 800 primitive ruins, Tonto National Monument and Tuzigoot National Monument help to satisfy the interest of visitors who have a special interest in such archeological treasures.

From the work of primitive peoples in Arizona it is scarcely more than a step to the space age probings of the scientific community at Kitt Peak National Observatory atop Kitt Peak on the Papago Indian Reservation. There, with some of the most advanced instruments in the world, galactic studies are opening up new space age vistas of the universe.

COMPAC-FACS

ARIZONA
The Grand Canyon State

HISTORY
Statehood: February 14, 1912
Admitted as: 48th state
Capital: Phoenix, settled 1867
OFFICIAL SYMBOLS
Motto: Ditat Deus (God enriches)
Bird: Cactus wren
Flower: Saguaro cactus blossom
Tree: Paloverde
Colors: Blue and old gold
Song: "Arizona" (a march)
GEO-FACS
Area: 114,000 sq. mi.
Rank in Area: 6th
Length (n/s): 392 mi.
Width (e/w): 338 mi.
Geographic Center: 55 mi. ese of Prescott
Highest Point: 12,633 ft. (Humphreys Peak)
Lowest Point: 70 ft. (Colorado River)
Mean Elevation: 4,100 ft.
Temperature, Extreme Range: 167 degrees
Number of Counties: 15
POPULATION
Total: 3,053,000 (1984)
Rank: 28th

THAT'S CURIOUS:
An adobe carving of a cat on one side of the San Xavier mission faces an adobe mouse on the other. Indian legend says that when the cat catches the mouse, the world will end.

The capitol complex with the winged statue of Liberty and Peace crowning the dome

Density: 26 persons per sq. mi.
Principal Cities: Phoenix, 789,704; Tucson, 330,537; Mesa, 152,453; Tempe, 106,743; Glendale, 97,172; Scottsdale, 86,622; Yuma, 42,481
EDUCATION
Schools: 867 elementary and secondary
Higher: 29
VITAL STATISTICS
Births (1980/83): 168,000
Deaths (1980/83): 71,000
Hospitals: 29
Drinking Age: 21
INTERESTING PEOPLE
Barry Goldwater, Cochise, Geronimo, Eusebio Francisco Kino, Francisco Tomas Garces, John Wesley Powell, Wyatt Earp, Oliver La Farge, Dick Wick Hall, Thomas Moran, Zane Grey, Morris Udall, Stewart Udall, Frank Lloyd Wright
WHEN DID IT HAPPEN?
1539: De Niza enters
1540: Coronado explores; Cardenas finds Grand Canyon
1580: Rodriguez begins mission work

1600: Franciscan missions commence
1680: Destruction of missions
1692: Kino undertakes mission work
1752: First permanent European settlement, Tubac
1768: Garces arrives at missions
1775: Tucson established
1781: Yuma Indians murder Garces
1822: Mexican revolution gains control
1848: U.S. controls most of present Arizona
1853: Arizona borders completed with Gadsden Purchase
1863: Arizona territory
1869: Powell runs Grand Canyon rapids
1881: Statewide rail line
1889: Capital located at Phoenix
1911: T. Roosevelt Dam dedicated by Roosevelt
1912: Statehood
1930: Coolidge dedicates Coolidge Dam
1936: Operations start at Hoover Dam
1964: Glen Canyon Dam operational
1975: Population growth leads the nation
1984: Reagan wins state vote; Democrats retain statehouse

COLORADO

FASCINATING COLORADO

"Colorado has it all," as someone remarked, "unsurpassed scenery ranging from the fertile plains through the most extensive mountain heights and canyon depths, with some of the most exciting cities of both the prehistoric past and the present."

However, the state's wealth, culture and beauty are matched by the facts and incidents which add human interest to its story.

History tells of the great civilization destroyed by ground corn, of the "unclimbable" mountain which is now scaled by more than 500,000 tenderfoot visitors each year, and the discovery of the square mile of antlers.

History recounts how one of the most beautiful of all state symbols was chosen by schoolchildren, and tells of the town that remained in the Confederacy for only a single day, of the portion of Colorado that did not join the United States until 1936, of the man who said "Go West, young man," and took his own suggestion.

The majestic aspects of geography are contrasted with such sidelights as the meaning of the thirteenth step on the state capitol, the geographic features that look like a gigantic corpse, the "Ivy League" mountains, the youthful mountains only 60 million years old, the mineral that helped to win a Nobel Prize, the name of the range inspired by the blood of Christ and the parks not made by man.

The fascinating people associated with Colorado include the woman who gained fame because she was inspired by the mountain view, the unsinkable Molly, the prospector who found a rich claim and spent his share in one night in a bar, and the man who would not donate a chandelier to a church because he could not "play" it.

All this, and much more, contribute to the fascination as well as the grandeur of Colorado.

THE FACE OF COLORADO

"O beautiful for spacious skies, for amber waves of grain, for purple mountain majesties...," wrote Katherine Lee Bates as she recalled the inspiration of her visit to the top of Pikes Peak. That view of Colorado inspired her anthem "America the Beautiful."

"Purple mountain majesties" certainly describes much of Colorado, with its average elevation a thousand feet higher than a mile. However, the state also has its "fruited plains," sloping gradually upward from east to west and covering almost half the state.

The plains end abruptly where the mountain foothills extend across the state from north to south. Here the North American Rockies stretch their widest and reach their highest average height. They wind and twist and loom over about a fourth of the entire area of the state.

The United States has 70 mountain peaks over 14,000 feet, and Colorado claims 53 of them. Over a thousand Colorado mountains soar above 10,000 feet. The mountains of Switzerland

would be swallowed up six times over by Colorado's peaks. The Front Range is one of the largest. It looms as a majestic backdrop behind several of Colorado's major cities. Loftiest of all the state's many ranges is the Sawatch.

Some of the ranges take their names from various characteristics. Mummy Range appears something like a gigantic corpse, and the winter months stretch out on the Never Summer Range. Individual mountain names are very imaginative, such as the three peaks named Princeton, Yale and Harvard.

Mt. Elbert is the highest peak in Colorado, but it is only about 13 feet higher than Mount Massive.

Colorado is completely spanned from north to south by the great Continental Divide. This divider of waters twists and turns so much that someone has said it resembles "a snake in agony."

Three of the nation's greatest rivers rise in the Colorado heights. Among the longest on the east slope are the Rio Grande—starting in the San Juan Mountains—and the Arkansas. Both eventually reach the Gulf of Mexico, but the Arkansas goes the long way around by way of the Mississippi River. Other rivers bound for the Mississippi are the Platte and the Republican.

Flowing in the opposite direction is one of the greatest rivers of the west. The Colorado has its tiny start in lofty Grand Lake, and before it ends in the Gulf of California it has provided life giving water for much of the entire southwest.

The tremendous snows of the mountains melt to provide water for a host of other rivers.

Opposite, Mile-high Denver

At 8,369 feet, Grand Lake is the largest high lake in the country. Many smaller lakes dot the countryside, including 200 on the top of Grand Mesa.

The western fourth of the state is known as the high mesa country. Grand Mesa is one of the outstanding geographical features of the west. These isolated mountains are known as "mesas" or "tables" because their upper parts have been cut off, and they have large flat tops. Grand Mesa is said to be the largest uplift of this kind in the world, covering 625 square miles.

Mesa country is carved by many deep canyons, including 2,500-foot-deep Black Canyon of the Gunnison River and yawning Yampa River Canyon.

In the far northwest, Colorado encompasses a small part of the Uinta Mountains.

Lovely but not as dramatic are the major valleys high in the Rockies. They are called "parks." Estes Park is the best known. San Louis is the largest of the parks; others are South Park, Middle Park and North Park.

Colorado is one of only two states with four straight manmade boundaries.

Prehistoric Colorado may once have been an almost-level plain. The last of the many forces of nature came about as the earth cooled and shrank, forcing up the Rocky Mountains. Because this happened "only" about 60,000,000 years ago, the Rockies are said to be the youngest of all the major mountains of the world.

Prehistoric times are also represented by some of the finest fossil beds anywhere. Dinosaur National Monument is noted as one of the most important sources of the remains of almost every

29

"In Mountain Heights, Colorado" by E. Martin Hennings

type of dinosaur known.

The high, dry climate of Colorado has been praised for its healthful qualities. Denver surprises many visitors with its generally mild and sunny climate.

EARLY DWELLERS

"A palace carved into a cliff!" That might have been the exclamation of Charlie Mason or Richard Wetherill in 1888 as they discovered the best known of all prehistoric dwellings in the United States. They were the first non-natives of record to stumble on the Cliff Palace in what is now Mesa Verde National Park.

The ruins of Mesa Verde are a striking example of the work of the Pueblo people who began to come into Colorado about 1100 years ago. They used rock and adobe construction to build very large and tall apartment houses. Many times, they were built in hollows high up on the sides of cliffs. This was done to make the approach difficult for their enemies.

Construction was generally of high quality, and often there were painted designs on the walls. These Pueblo people grew corn, squash and other crops on land watered by skillfully engineered irrigation systems.

Each cluster of dwellings had religious centers called kivas, and some communities had temples set aside entirely for religious use.

No one is sure why their civilization died out, but the great drought beginning in 1276 A.D. probably was a principal reason.

Earlier prehistoric peoples included hunters of perhaps 30,000 years ago. Their stone weapon points have been found in the remains of very early animals.

Later, the Basketmakers wove many fine articles out of branches or rushes or reed. Even some of their houses were of woven construction. The Pueblo people may have evolved from these people, building on their weaving, pottery, gardening and other skills.

When Europeans first visited the area, the Ute Indians were the largest

THAT'S CURIOUS:
Spanish explorer Valverde looked up from the valley of the Purgatoire River just before dawn. At that moment the sun bathed the mountains in a red glow. He exclaimed "Sangre de Cristo" (blood of Christ), and that range has been the Sangre de Cristo ever since.

group inhabiting present Colorado. They roamed the mountain valleys, high mesas and even parts of the southern plains. Later Indian groups were the Indians of the plains—Kiowa, Arapahoe, Cheyenne and Comanche. Sioux and Pawnee groups also came and went.

The plains Indians seldom built permanent homes but roamed about, living in tepees and gaining food and clothing by hunting.

Many of the plains groups were very superstitious. If a leader died, they would all leave the death place and move elsewhere.

STIRRINGS

Although Europeans may have visited present Colorado before 1694, the first written account was made in that year by Diego de Vargas as he searched for slaves who had escaped from Taos in the south. The slaves were recaptured in 1706 by Juan Ulibarri. When he discovered that French trappers had preceded him there, he quickly claimed the area for Spain.

As time went by, missionaries and explorers visited the region and left Spanish names at many locations.

After Spain gave up all claim to the Louisiana Territory, the boundaries of lands still claimed by Spain were disputed. A few Spanish gold prospectors and traders had operated in the San Luis Valley, and Spanish interests centered there.

When the U.S. purchased Louisiana Territory in 1803, little time was lost in sending Lieutenant Zebulon Pike to explore the southern portion of that area. In 1806 Pike and his party moved up the Arkansas River and soon saw a distant mountain. That mountain is now known as Pikes Peak in the explorer's honor. He wrongly estimated that it was 18,000 feet high and said it could never be climbed.

The explorers visited Royal Gorge and South Park, went south into San Luis Valley and were arrested by Spanish authorities who still claimed the area.

In 1819 the boundary was established as running up the Arkansas River to the Continental Divide and following the divide north. In 1820 Major Stephen H. Long explored the area with scientist Dr. Edwin James.

EARLY GROWTH

When Mexico tore away from Spain, the new country encouraged trade with their settlements centered at Santa Fe in present New Mexico. The trail from Missouri to Santa Fe was blazed, and it cut across southeastern Colorado. Thousands of American traders followed the trail; trappers came in to hunt furs.

Established in 1828 by the Bent and St. Vrain trading firm, Fort Bent soon became headquarters for the entire mountain/plains area around present La Junta.

Fort Lupton became the first permanent outpost in present northern Colo-

Great Sand Dunes National Monument

Bust." Unfortunately for most, it was "bust" since there seemed to be little gold, and many returned over "starvation trail."

Then in May, 1859, John Gregory actually did find what came to be called the richest mile on earth, and the boom town of Central City sprang up almost overnight in Gregory Gulch. By winter there were probably 10,000 eager gold seekers in that area.

The lack of formal government caused many difficulties with outlaws and claim-jumpers. Finally, in 1861, Congress organized the territory.

The Confederate flag flew over Denver for one day, but the Confederate sympathizers backed down. Many volunteers joined the Union army from frontier Colorado. No Civil War battles were fought there, but Indian troubles were an almost-constant threat through the decade, beginning in 1861. Settlers, wagon trains and stagecoaches were attacked. When the Cheyenne and Arapahoe did not receive treaty monies promised them, they joined the attack.

Government forces finally were brought in, and in one of the many sad incidents of cruelty to the Indians, 500 were killed, said to be mostly women and children.

The united plains Indians naturally responded with fierce reprisals over a long period. Government forces fought many skirmishes and two battles before the Indians were finally subdued, and most of the Indians were harshly moved to reservations in Oklahoma.

Statehood bills passed by Congress in

rado. A rival trading company set up Fort St. Vrain near Gilcrest in 1838, and it became the center of Rocky Mountain activity.

In 1840 the Arapahoe, Cheyenne, Comanche and Kiowa signed a treaty of peace and mutual defense which was generally kept. Pueblo was founded in 1842 by Jim Beckwourth, and four years later Mexico gave up all claim to any part of Colorado. Parts of Colorado claimed by Texas were given up in 1850, and the state gained its present boundaries. Denver was founded in 1858.

In 1858 rumors of rich gold brought thousands of fortune hunters to Cherry Creek with the slogan of "Pikes Peak or

THAT'S CURIOUS:
Only 14 years after Pike said his mountain could not be climbed, Dr. Edwin James led a party to the top.

1866 and 1867 were vetoed by President Andrew Johnson. In 1876 statehood finally was authorized, and Colorado became the "Centennial State," arriving just 100 years after U.S. independence.

Colorado gold had almost died out when silver was discovered near Leadville, and another rush began, bringing 30,000 hopefuls and making Leadville into one of the most legendary of all the mining boom towns across the country, complete with saloons, outlaws and gunfights.

UP-TO-DATE

In 1879 Indian troubles erupted again with uprisings by the Ute against the injustices of Indian Agent Nathan C. Meeker. Meeker was killed, and the Ute called for peace, but in 1887 they again tried desperately to win back their ancestral lands, only to be subdued once more and taken to Utah.

Earlier gold searches had seemed to prove the Cripple Creek area worthless until 1891, when cowboy Robert Womack discovered a rich claim, sold it almost immediately for $500, and spent most of it the same night. The gold which has come from Cripple Creek mines has produced more wealth than any other except for the Witwatersrand mines of South Africa.

Women were granted the vote in Colorado in 1893.

The Festival of Mountain and Plain in 1895 attracted much attention to Denver; a different kind of attention came with the killing of the last wild buffalo in the state two years later. These were perhaps the last wild buffalo left in the nation.

Denver entertained the national Democratic Convention in 1908, and the Republicans responded by sending President Theodore Roosevelt to dedicate the first Reclamation Bureau project that same year.

World War I called 43,000 to service from Colorado, and 1,000 were killed in that conflict.

A disastrous flood at Pueblo in 1921 and robberies at the Denver mint and a Lamar bank highlighted the 1920's.

Colorado celebrated the completion of the world's highest suspension bridge when the Royal Gorge was spanned in 1929.

Duststorms, drought and depression were the three D's of the 1930's. "Part of my farm blew off into Kansas yesterday, so I guess I'll have to pay taxes there, too," one farmer lamented. However, rains finally brought relief; soil conservation took a firm hold, and much of the damage to the land was repaired.

World War II brought 138,832 into service from Colorado, and 2,700 lost their lives.

By 1965 North American Air Defense Command (NORAD) had completed its installation deep in Cheyenne Mountain, where it became the heart of the continent's defense system.

During the 1970's and 80's, Colorado prosperity was emphasized by the enormous growth of Denver, including new skyscrapers over 50 stories high built in the period 1980-85. A new heritage center, skywalks and bridges, vast new shopping malls and shopping centers and high-tech operations contributed to the renewal of the city in the same period. Colorado also has enjoyed the establishment of headquarters of great corporations.

PEOPLES

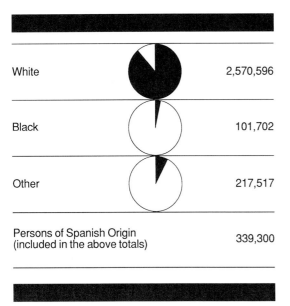

White	2,570,596
Black	101,702
Other	217,517
Persons of Spanish Origin (included in the above totals)	339,300

In 1986 the suburb of Aurora became the fastest growing of all the top 100 cities of the country.

PERSONALITIES

President Chester Arthur attended the second wedding of this Colorado man in Washington, who built a million dollar grand opera house at Denver and also donated a fine opera house at Leadville. He tossed handfuls of silver dollars to the stars on the stage in both towns. This generous giver was H.A.W. Tabor. He and his first wife, Augusta, came to Colorado during the first gold boom. Unsuccessful at first, he grubstaked some successful miners and invested his share so successfully that he became very wealthy.

Tabor became a politician, served as Colorado's lieutenant governor and as a U.S. Senator to fill an unexpired term.

Augusta Tabor was much admired in Colorado, but after Tabor had gained wealth and high living, he considered her to be dull and divorced her. He then married Mary Elizabeth McCourt Doe. Everyone called this lovely second wife Baby Doe.

Together they went through the Tabor wealth almost as fast as it came in. When he died penniless, he is supposed to have said to Baby Doe, "Hang on to the Matchless." That was the mine from which much of the wealth had come.

Baby Doe lived on in a shack on their claim, never accepting offers of help. She became a pathetic, familiar figure, trying to interest people in the mine. She never sold the Matchless and died in her shack in 1935.

Some of the other mine fortunes were squandered, including that of Jack Morrisey, who died in a Denver poorhouse.

However, Spencer Penrose, who made his fortune in gold at Cripple Creek, invested it wisely and continued to be successful. He built the Broadmoor Hotel at Colorado Springs. His wife Julia, used great style and taste in the hotel's design and furnishings, and the resort is still considered one of the most elegant in the nation.

THAT'S CURIOUS:
Some Coloradans, perhaps with tongue in cheek, claimed that South Park had never been made a part of the U.S. because it was not a part of either Spanish claims or the Louisiana Purchase. Governor E.C. Johnson took part in a colorful ceremony in 1936 which brought the park into the national fold.

Penrose financed the construction of the road up Pikes Peak and constructed the Shrine to the Sun on Cheyenne Mountain, which he dedicated to the memory of his friend Will Rogers. He had a personal collection of animals, which grew until it became the Cheyenne Mountain Zoo.

Another mining tycoon, Thomas F. Walsh, both made and lost a fortune at Leadville. However, the fortune he made at Ouray was even larger. His daughter, Evelyn Walsh McLean, became a prominent leader of society; she wrote a biography of her father.

Perhaps the most successful of all the Colorado tycoons were John F. Campion and Winfield Scott Stratton. Campion struck it rich in gold mining, then began Colorado's first large-scale sugar beet refining. Samuel Newhouse started with a Leadville fortune and became a copper baron. He named world leaders among his friends and was called "the Midas of the Rockies."

Newspaper magnate Horace Greeley's famous quotation about going west was one he himself took seriously. He spent some time in Colorado. Then he sent his editor and partner, Nathan C. Meeker, to lead a group of settlers in Colorado. They managed to build 35 houses and other structures within two weeks of arriving at the Cache la Poudre River. Meeker was killed by the Indians, but the community prospered and took the name Greeley, for the founder.

Another well-known name in Colorado is that of David Moffat. He built a railroad over the Rockies, and his name became attached to the well-known Moffet Tunnel.

Still another name associated with Colorado is that of George Engelman, a botanist whose name is borne by the Engelman spruce.

David May is known across the country for the famous chain of department stores bearing his name. His first store was started at Leadville.

Novelist Helen Hunt Jackson, poet Eugene Field and Zane Grey, one of the most famous authors of western novels, all had Colorado associations.

Artist Albert Bierstadt was especially well known for his brilliant paintings of Rocky Mountain scenes, many of which hang in the most distinguished museums.

Christopher "Kit" Carson was the best known and most successful of all the frontier scouts. Much of his time was spent exploring and guiding parties in Colorado.

William "Buffalo Bill" Cody also had many Colorado associations, and many visitors view his grave on Lookout Mountain.

Jazz king, Paul Whiteman; broadcast personality, Lowell Thomas; astronaut Scott Carpenter; heavyweight champion, Jack Dempsey; and Supreme Court Justice Byron R. White, all have Colorado roots.

THAT'S CURIOUS:
One of the mining tycoons, Auguste Rische, donated money for a church. Someone suggested that a large chandelier would improve the sanctuary. Rische replied that it would be a foolish investment; he did not know how to play a chandelier, and he didn't think anyone else did either.

A WEALTH OF NATURE

Gold and silver and other minerals have already brought much wealth to Colorado. However, others of the more than 450 useful minerals found in the state will probably bring even greater revenue.

One of the greatest reserves for an oil-hungry world will undoubtedly be recovered some day from the vast shale beds of Colorado. These shale rocks are said to contain five times more oil than all the world's present liquid reserves. At present, shale cannot be removed profitably, but greater demand and new methods will someday bring this treasure into full use.

Colorado has the largest reserves of coal in the country. Colorado also possesses two-thirds of the known supply of molybdenum worldwide. Alabaster and a wide range of gemstones may also be found in the state.

The one mineral in short supply is water. Precipitation is light on the average, and most of the moisture comes as snowfall in the mountains. Much of it melts in summer and runs into the west-flowing streams, but the greatest need is on the east side of the mountains. To bring the waters where they are needed, great tunnels and other vast engineering efforts have succeeded, beginning in 1959 with the Colorado-Big Thompson project. This was only the first of several such gigantic projects. The western streams also have been dammed, making large lakes to supply irrigation projects.

Animal life in Colorado is varied and often delightful. Explorer Coronado wrote about the horns of the bighorn sheep, "...the size of which was something to marvel at." Among the animal oddities is the ring-tailed cat, said to have the tail of a raccoon, the front feet of a cat, with the body of a squirrel and the head and cry of a fox.

The "haymaker of the heights" is one description of the pika, because the little animal stores grass in miniature haystacks for use during the long winter.

The state flower of Colorado, the columbine, was chosen by the school-children of the state in 1899. This breathtakingly beautiful blue flower can reach a spread of three inches across a single blossom.

USING THE WEALTH

Carnotite from Colorado was used by the Curies in their discovery of radium. Similarly, the world's first atomic bomb was made from Colorado uranium, still yielding mineral income to the state.

Sixty percent of the world's molybdenum comes from Colorado. This is a vital mineral used in hardening steel. Seventy-five percent of U.S. vanadium is also produced in Colorado.

Milling and smelting of ores continues to be an important state industry, particularly in steel.

The minerals of the state provide a market for the large production of mining equipment and machinery, and Denver is said to be the largest producer of such products in the world.

The state's agricultural products are also widely processed by Colorado manufacturers, including beet sugar production.

San Juan County is one of the few in the U.S. without a single acre cultivated. In striking contrast, Weld County is ranked among the top ten richest agricultural counties in the nation. Livestock is the biggest single producer of the state's agricultural income. Greeley has the world's largest feed lots. San Luis Valley is known for its pea-fed hogs. Wheat is the principal field crop, followed by hay, sorghum, broom corn and potatoes.

When the stagecoach arrived at Canon one day, the newspaper noted that among its passengers were several bodies. Long past are the days of highway robbers and of wagons careening down steep slopes with no wagon brakes. The pioneering spirit of transportation is evident in the railroads that spanned the impossible mountains and in Mount Evans Highway, which brings vehicles to the second highest road in the world. The magnificent Trail Ridge Road is the country's highest cross-country highway.

GETTING AROUND

Denver is the starting point for dozens of fascinating and varied one-day tours. One of the most interesting is called Gateway to Gold. One of the most interesting points on this tour, Central City, is a National Historic District and looks much as it did a hundred years ago. The buildings have formed the backdrop

THE ECONOMY

in millions of $

Manufacturing	17,213
Service	7,325
Tourism	4,000
Agriculture	2,927
Mining	2,678

Principal Products:
food, instruments, machinery (except electrical)

Agriculture:
cattle, wheat, corn, dairy products

for several movies. The old opera house is still used for performances, and visitors can still tour two mines.

The dirt road from Central City to Idaho Springs twists and turns above such yawning canyons that it is known as the "Oh, My God Road." The 14-mile highway to the summit of Mt. Evans is the highest paved road in the nation and second in height only to Mintaka Pass in China. Idaho Springs was the state's first major gold strike center, and visitors may still pan for gold there. Georgetown has over 200 restored Victorian buildings. Each summer, the narrow-gauge steam locomotives are fired up to travel the Georgetown Loop railroad. Building this

THAT'S CURIOUS:

The grassy pastures of the Colorado parks provided such good food that large grass-eaters were abundant. English authoress, Isabella Bird, wrote that she saw a square mile of Estes Park covered with the cast off antlers of elk.

Tabor Opera House, Leadville

road was one of the most difficult railroad construction jobs ever undertaken.

Perhaps the most traveled route out of Denver is the great circle to Rocky Mountain National Park and back. Quaint Estes Park is the major resort village for the area. It is often named as one of the 10 most interesting small towns in the country. From Estes, Trail Ridge Road, the highest continuous highway in the world, crosses the Continental Divide at 12,183 feet. Beautiful Grand Lake is the world's highest yacht anchorage; on its shores nestles another interesting tourist village.

Berthoud Pass is the highest pass in the state that remains open all winter.

A different kind of one-day trip from Denver takes the visitor to Pikes Peak country. Self-guided tours allow the visitor to see the Air Force Academy with its famous chapel. Near Manitou Springs is the Garden of the Gods, containing spectacular natural sculptures carved from the brilliant red rocks.

Pikes Peak can be ascended by car, by the world's highest cog railroad or on foot or by horseback. Colorado Springs is a center for visiting the Garden of the Gods, Will Rogers Shrine to the Sun, Seven Falls, Cheyenne Mountain Zoo and the historic mining town of Cripple Creek.

Near Canyon City, the world's highest suspension bridge sways 1,053 feet above the roaring Arkansas River. The bottom of the canyon can be reached by the world's steepest incline railroad. Pueblo is the site of Colorado's State Fair.

Central Colorado is known as the

"Crown Jewel of the Rockies."

Glenwood Springs centers its vacation opportunities around the warm mineral waters. The picturesque silver mining town of Aspen has been transformed into an internationally famed cultural center, home of many famous entertainers and jet-setters. Some call Aspen America's best-known ski area, but Colorado also has dozens of other ski areas with outstanding facilities.

At Leadville the Tabor Opera House, Augusta Tabor cottage, Baby Doe cabin and the Matchless Mine are all haunting reminders of the historic past. Climax produces three-fifths of the world's molybdenum. Encircled by the mighty mountains, Vail Village is a magnificent year-round resort.

In southwest Colorado, Europeans have lived at St. Luis longer than anywhere else in Colorado, but prehistoric people at Mesa Verde National Park long preceded them. In the pit dwellings of the Basketmakers, the scroll of time unrolls to 1 A.D.

From Durango, visitors ride the rails into yesterday aboard the narrow-gauge railroad to Silverton, the Old West locale of many movie westerns.

Great Sand Dunes National Monument near Alamosa stretches across 57 square miles of glistening white sand. Black Canyon of the Gunnison National Monument preserves the area which plunges 2,800 feet to the churning river.

Northwest is Dinosaurland. Dinosaur National Monument offers one of the most effectively displayed exhibits of the remains of those great creatures. Glenwood Springs boasts the world's largest natural hot springs swimming pool.

The thirteenth step of the capitol at Denver is exactly one mile high. The building's huge murals and hall of fame portraits of pioneers in stained glass are principal features of the building, which was completed in 1900.

Larimer Square and Heritage Square are restored sections of the city, reminders of the historic past, as is the Brown House, home of the "Unsinkable Molly."

More spectacular is modern Denver with 16 new skyscrapers downtown, vast new hotels, and a new 80-million dollar performing arts center which has three theaters, a film center and the nation's first symphony hall in-the-round, home of the Denver Symphony.

A new mile-long 16th Street Mall and two new downtown shopping centers make the city one of the finest anywhere for shoppers.

The new Colorado Heritage Center and a new Museum of Western Art enhance the city's attractions.

Five billion coins a year are produced at the Denver branch of the U.S. Mint. Visitors may take an exciting 20-minute tour of the mint.

Outside Denver, Red Rocks Amphitheatre provides outdoor seating for 8,000 in a setting among the high red sandstone rocks. Summer concerts feature performances ranging from the hardest rock music to the great symphonies.

Buffalo Bill's Grave and Museum honors the exploits of the frontier scout and showman. From the grave site above Denver, the panoramic view highlights the Mile-High city.

COMPAC-FACS
COLORADO
Centennial State

HISTORY
Statehood: August 1, 1876
Admitted as: 38th state

39

The mile-high step is one of those leading to the capitol

Capital: Denver, founded 1858
OFFICIAL SYMBOLS
Motto: Nil sine Numine (Nothing without Providence)
Animal: Bighorn sheep (ovis canadensis candensis)
Bird: Lark bunting (calamospiza melanocorys stejneger)
Flower: Rocky Mountain columbine (aquilegia caerules)
Tree: Colorado blue spruce (picea pungens)
Gem: Aquamarine
Fossil: Stegosaurus
Colors: Blue and white
Song: "Where the Columbines Grow"
GEO-FACS
Area: 104,091 sq. mi.
Rank in Area: 8th
Length (n/s): 275 mi.
Width (e/w): 387 mi.
Geographic Center: In Park Co., 30 mi. nw of Pikes Peak
Highest Point: 14,433 ft. (Mt. Elbert)
Lowest Point: 3,350 ft. (Arkansas River)

Mean Elevation: 6,800 ft.
Temperature, Extreme Range: 179 degrees
Number of Counties: 63
POPULATION
Total: 3,178,000 (1984)
Rank: 26th
Density: 30.6 persons per sq. mi.
Principal Cities: Denver, 492,365; Colorado Springs, 214,821; Aurora, 158,588; Lakewood, 113,808; Pueblo, 101,686; Arvada, 84,576; Boulder, 76,685
EDUCATION
Schools: 1,271 elementary and secondary
Higher: 47
VITAL STATISTICS
Births (1980/83): 172,000
Deaths (1980/83): 64,000
Hospitals: 97
Drinking Age: 21 (18, limited purchase)
INTERESTING PEOPLE
Byron R. White, Paul Whiteman, H.A.W. Tabor, Augusta Tabor, Mary Elizabeth (Baby Doe) Tabor, Spencer Penrose, Thomas F. Walsh, Evelyn Walsh McLean, John F. Campion, Winfield Scott Stratton, Horace Greeley, David Moffat, George Engelman, David May, Helen Hunt Jackson, Eugene Field, Zane Grey, Albert Bierstadt, Christopher (Kit) Carson, M. Scott Carpenter, Jack Dempsey, William (Buffalo Bill) Cody
WHEN DID IT HAPPEN?
1682: France claims part of present Colorado
1694: Diego de Vargas explores
1776: Escalante and Dominguez discover Mesa Verde
1801: Spain relinquishes claim to eastern plains
1803: U.S. acquires eastern plains
1806: Zebulon Pike expedition
1819: Boundary established on southwest
1820: Pikes Peak climbed
1828: Bents Fort started
1850: U.S. completes acquisition of Colorado
1858: Denver founded; gold rush commences
1861: Colorado Territory
1876: Statehood
1891: Gold strike at Cripple Creek
1908: Denver, Democratic Nat. Convention
1917: World War I claims 1,009 Colorado lives
1929: Suspension bridge spans Royal Gorge
1941: World War II claims 2,700 Colorado lives
1965: North American Air Defense Command Center opens
1986: Aurora is America's fastest-growing city

IDAHO

FASCINATING IDAHO

"I discovered immense ranges of high mountains still to the west of us with their tops partially covered with snow. I now descended the mountain about 3/4 of a mile which I found much steeper than on the opposite side, to a handsome bold running Creek of cold Clear water...I first tasted the water of the great Columbia River..."

This part of the journal of Meriwether Lewis, leader of the first American overland expedition to the Pacific Ocean, may have been the first written description of the region now called Idaho.

Still to be found at a much later date were the deepest canyon, the underground rivers that rumbled, the upside-down river, the eccentric bear and the lava tree-molds.

The expedition encountered many natural and manmade wonders, but perhaps they did not see the birds with the reverse roles or the large work of art. They may have heard the Indians tell of the "sun coming down the mountains." They did witness the unbelievable reunion and watched in horror as the hostess cut her wrists, and they did say with real conviction that they had encountered "the noblest tribe of all."

Still to come were the exhausted travelers, dying of thirst, who could not reach the water only a mile and a half away, the "a palousey" horses, the tilting combines, the mystery of the anonymous salmon and the naturally heated homes."

By the time Europeans reached the land known today as Idaho, the time had long passed when the north was frozen cold and the south was red hot. However, what they did find was a land of vast variety and scenic beauty, of lovely lakes, unbelievably fertile hills, and some of the noblest Indians (as well as some of the most fierce)—a land that today lives in a measure of peace and harmony probably unsurpassed anywhere.

THE FACE OF IDAHO

By the time Idaho's borders were formed, boundaries of the surrounding states had already been fixed. That is the reason given for the state's rather strange shape, tapering up into a panhandle that touches British Columbia, Canada, on the north.

The bordering states are Washington, Oregon, Nevada, Utah, Wyoming and Montana. The mountain border along the crest of the Bitterroot Range and the section of the western border following the Snake River are the only natural borders; the other borders are manmade.

The Snake is one of Idaho's many unique rivers. The French called the Snake the "Accursed Mad River" because of its many inhospitable shores and its many twists and turns. The Snake enters Idaho flowing northwest, then turns southwest, swerves to the northwest,

THAT'S CURIOUS:

Unfortunate travelers, dying of thirst at Hell's Canyon, could look down longingly at the waters of the Snake River but had no way of descending to the bottom, to save their lives.

41

heads northeast, then northwest again, and finally flows almost due north before leaving Idaho.

In its northeast section, the Snake has carved the deepest canyon on the North American continent. Hell's Canyon descends almost 8,000 feet from the top of He Devil Mountain to the depths of the canyon.

The principal tributary of the Snake, the Salmon, starts from the Sawtooth Mountains on a northerly course; it too turns west and south. Its tributaries are major rivers in themselves. The Salmon has been called The "River of No Return" because the waters would carry a boatman downstream, but he could never return up the treacherous rapids against the swift flowing current.

Another of Idaho's eccentric rivers is the Bear, which starts in Utah, enters Wyoming, then turns into Idaho, flows in an arc within the state, then returns to enter Great Salt Lake in Utah. The Bear occupies much of the region of Idaho which is in the Great Basin. Here no rivers drain into the sea, but all flow into some part of the basin.

For almost 450 miles within Idaho, the Snake has only one river flowing into it, the Malad River. Although the Malad flows with the volume of a river, it is only three miles long and has been called the shortest river in the world.

Many rivers in various parts of the world flow underground for part or all of their course. The Lost River area probably has more of them than any region of similar size. The vast stretches of volcanic rocks swallow up the rivers of the region, where they sometimes flow for hundreds of miles below ground. It is said

Opposite, Boise

that in certain areas a visitor with an ear to the ground can hear the waters rumbling below the surface. The Lost River comes to light in a spectacular way when it surges out of the cliff from hundreds of openings to flow into the Snake River. This is the Thousand Springs.

The St. Joe River also has a nickname, the "Highest Navigable River in the World." The more than 2,000 lakes in Idaho extend from Upper Priest Lake in the northwest corner to Bear Lake, shared with Utah, in the southwest corner of Idaho. The natural lakes in the panhandle are said to rank among the loveliest in the world. Beautiful Lake Pend Oreille is the largest of them. The Snake River has been dammed at spots; the largest artificial lake is American Falls Reservoir, stretching north from a dam near American Falls.

The Shoshone term "ee-da-how" is an exclamation meaning "behold the sun coming down the mountain." It gives the state its name. The state has 22 distinct mountain ranges upon which the sun often does "come down." Residents say that if their state could be flattened out, it would rival Texas for size. The Bitterroot and Sawtooth are two of the largest mountain groups. The mountains do not reach the great heights of other mountain states, but they are noted for their craggy and rugged appearance, with the Sawtooth the most rugged in the northwest United States.

Perhaps the most spectacular of all Idaho natural features was formed in a prehistoric period, ending at about the time of the fall of Rome. For unknown ages lava poured from the ground in such volume that huge unmelted stones were carried up and deposited like corks on water. The unbelievable quantity of molten rock that spewed forth covered an area of 200,000 square miles to a depth not yet determined in some areas.

A portion of this great flow has been preserved in Craters of the Moon National Monument, resembling the ruptured lunar surface. In this relatively small part of the lava area, there are 63 volcanic craters, innumerable lava and cinder cones and flowholes, or fumeroles. The lava has flowed into innumerable forms—twisted ropes, great sheets like folded paper, blisters where lava bubbles burst, vast dimpled "waffles" and branches like coral. Almost every color can be seen in the lava flow, including the exotic deep cobalt blue of the Dragon flow.

Some of the lava was dashed so high into the air that it cooled as it fell to earth and formed gigantic balls. Some areas look as if they were covered with light foam and froth instead of lava. In some places whole forests were evaporated, leaving holes where the trunks once stood. These holes form perfect molds of the vanished trees.

Less dramatic lava flows, known as fissure eruptions, provided the layers of lava which underlie the Palouse area in western central Idaho. Over the years the winds brought silt to cover the Palouse with a deep, rich layer of soil known as loess.

Much earlier in prehistoric time, forces even greater than the volcanoes pushed up one of the world's largest masses of granite, known as the Idaho Batholith, a solid block about 80 miles across, extending from St. Joe River to the Snake River Plain. This "most notable geologic feature of the state" has the scientific name Cretacean Uplift.

Strangely, during much of the time that the south was red hot, the north was covered with three of the four great frozen sheets of the glacial age. When the ice melted, it backed up at present Coeur d'Alene to form prehistoric Lake Missoula; the waters then rushed out with a great flow that caused a mammoth waterfall, now Dry Falls in Washington.

Southern Idaho had a small part of a vast prehistoric lake of its own—Lake Bonneville, covering 20,000 square miles. The waters of this lake diverted into the Snake River, and only Utah's Great Salt Lake remains of this former monster lake.

Prehistoric animal remains are common in Idaho. Perhaps the most unusual has been the fossil of a horse or zebra, the largest ever discovered, found in the Snake River Valley in 1932. The site is the largest locale of prehistoric horse fossils known.

Another unusual fossil was that of a buffalo with seven-foot horns. Huge musk ox, mammoths and mastodons are among the many fossils, which also include the remains of a kind of cat not yet identified.

Fossil trees turned into charcoal by volcanic action have been found, as well as fossilized redwood, cypress and other trees not now growing in the area.

Prevailing Pacific Ocean winds help to keep the Idaho climate rather mild in both winter and summer, and the mountains are placed in such a way that most of the bitter winds from Canada are kept away.

EARLY DWELLERS

The earth shook; the ground rumbled, and white-hot molton volcanic rock flew into the air. The people must have fled in terror, but few if any could have escaped. Because of the arrowheads and other relics they left behind, it is known that people lived in the area at the time of the volcanic action which covered so much of present Idaho.

Of course, people had lived in the Idaho region for a much longer time, for at least 12,000 years and probably longer. Places of habitation at least 12,000 years old have have been found at Ebenezer Bar on the Salmon River near Shoup. Remnants of a tribe apparently related to the Pueblo people have been found near Marsing.

A find in 1933 included evidence of a civilization of about 3,000 years ago. Items made of wood not found in the area now, a brush of grasses tied together, skillfully woven bed mats and other household objects have been found near the mouth of the Salmon River.

A large lava rock on the Snake River south of Nampa preserves the largest prehistoric work of art ever found in the U.S. There are other fine pictographs (paintings) and petroglyphs (carvings) in cliffs and on rocks in other parts of the present state.

Of the Indians found by early European explorers, the Nez Perce have been

Chief Joseph The Younger of the Nez Perce

called "the noblest tribe of all." To the north also lived the Skitswish, Coeur d'Alene and Kootenai. Shoshone and Bannock were the warlike tribes of the present southern part of the state.

When the French first came into contact with the Coeur d'Alene, they found them to be docile but mean-spirited and shrewd in trading, so they gave them their French name which means "the heart of an awl."

The Kootanai are thought to have been the smallest of the 59 major-language families of native U.S. Americans.

The Shoshone were nicknamed the Snake, some say because they carried canes with carved serpent heads to frighten the plains Indians, who often were terrified by them.

The Shoshone groups that killed and

ate the mountain sheep were known as Sheepeaters, but they just as often ate the wonderful fresh salmon when they were available. After they had acquired horses, some of these sheepeaters went over to the plains to hunt buffalo and were called Lemhi.

Relatives of the Pend Oreille and the Coeur d'Alene were known as Flatheads, because they compressed the heads of infants to make them flat.

The northern tribes were very dependent on the salmon because hunting in the region was not good. After the salmon run, as much salmon as possible was dried for future use.

Some deer, mountain sheep, elk and other game were available to the southern tribesmen. All of the Indians of the area depended on berries and roots, especially the camas plant bulb, which was ground into flour.

Many of the horses of the early Spanish exploring parties either strayed away or were stolen by the Indians. By the time the Europeans came to present Idaho, the Indians of the region probably owned the greatest number of horses on the continent, including the spotted appaloosa, a beautiful and intelligent horse, much improved by the Indians over the years, especially by the Nez Perce.

In 1805, when the great explorers Lewis and Clark reached the crest of the Rockies, they went ahead into Idaho with a scouting party and met Chief Cameahwait. Their guide was the Indian woman Sacajawea, who had been kidnapped from the region by eastern tribes. When the scouting party returned to the main party, they discovered that by strange coincidence, Chief Cameahwait was Sacajawea's brother, and brother and sister were lovingly reunited.

After the entire party crossed into Idaho, they described many fascinating encounters with the Indians. As they continued west, the worst part of the whole exploration was endured in the stretch over the mountains between Lolo and the Clearwater River. As Clark wrote, "...not any of us have yet forgotten our sufferings in those mts in September last, I think it probable we never shall."

Next, they met the "handsome" and "very dressy" Nez Perce. They encountered the peculiar custom known as potlach. During the potlach parties, the host or hostess would try to give away all of his or her possessions. When one of the exploring party refused a gift, the woman who offered it cut her wrists.

At last, the group came to the Snake River at present Lewiston, travelled down the river and out of Idaho.

On the return trip, the party had to wait for the snows to melt, and Clark was kept busy treating the sickness and wounds of the Indians, who thought him a great medicine man. One of his accomplishments was to help an Indian chief recover from paralysis. The travelers spoke very highly of the Nez Perce as the only truly hospitable people they had met on their journey.

THAT'S CURIOUS:

Early settlers came to the region known as the Palouse. When they saw Indians riding by on their spotted horses, they remarked "That's a palousey." Eventually, the words were put together and became appaloosa, giving the breed its odd name.

EARLY GROWTH

The Lewis and Clark party left Idaho in June, 1806.

Three years later, explorer-businessman David Thompson built the first European-style building in present Idaho, called Kullyspell House, as a center for the Hudson's Bay Company fur trade.

The fur business prospered. In 1819 Donald Mackenzie brought the fur traders and Indians together in Boise Valley for the first great Rendezvous there. These were held annually at different places.

Fort Hall, built by Nathaniel Wyeth in 1834, was bought by the Hudson's Bay Trading Company and flourished, along with old Fort Boise, for 22 years.

The Reverend Jason Lee conducted Idaho's first religious service in 1834, and he set up the Lapwai Mission in 1836, near present Lewiston. He taught the Indians farming practices, milling and printing, in addition to the Christian religion.

Other missions were established, including Sacred Heart Mission, founded by Father Pierre Jean De Smet, first at Saint Maries in 1842; then it was moved to Cataldo in 1846.

Beginning in the mid-1840's, the huge migration to Oregon country brought thousands along the Oregon Trail across the present southeast corner of Idaho, crossing the Snake River at present Pocatello and into Oregon. Some of the pioneer ruts may still be seen.

Even more awesome was the rush of gold seekers, the 49'ers, on the way to California.

Indian troubles were followed by Indian agreements to remain on reservations in portions of Idaho, Oregon and Washington.

Idaho's first permanent settlement was Franklin, founded by the Mormons in 1860. They brought a 5-ton steam engine overland to power a sawmill at Franklin.

In that year gold was discovered by E. A. Pierce, and the town of Pierce grew up with all the rip-roaring life of so many other western mining towns.

Idaho Territory was established in 1863, and the capital moved to Boise in 1864.

As more settlers came in, the rich Indian lands looked even more attractive. Chief Joseph of the Nez Perce was forced to agree to move, but his people revolted, and the friendly Nez Perce went to war for the first time, in 1877. They soundly defeated Captain David Perry in the Battle of White Canyon on June 17, 1877. Then the Indians were defeated near Kamiah and decided to try to make their way to sanctuary in Canada. They crossed uninhabited parts of Idaho and left at Lolo Pass.

War with the Bannock Indians and an attempt to round up the Sheepeater peoples eventually brought Indian troubles to an end.

THAT'S CURIOUS:

A pioneer settler in the Palouse country told of the Nez Perce Indian father and his children who were given a meal in the settler's home. The next year during the salmon season, a large fish was laid anonymously at his doorstep. "As long as we lived there, we always got a salmon at the same time each year."

UP-TO-DATE

Gold, lead, zinc and silver strikes brought in many miners; then a railroad and the first telephone arrived in 1883. The silver-lead-zinc strike at Coeur d'Alene in 1884 began the far-spreading operations in what is still the leading mining area of Idaho.

July 3, 1890, brought statehood with a thunderous July 4th celebration the next day.

In 1899 the miners of the Coeur d'Alene district started one of the country's bitterest strikes. Mine machinery and buildings were destroyed, and the U.S. Army finally had to come in to bring order.

In 1905 Frank Steunenberg, who was governor during the strikes, was murdered by a bomb explosion. The trial for his murder in 1907 proved to be one of the most publicized in the country's history.

Craters of the Moon National Monument was established in 1924, and in 1929 David Thompson's Kullyspell House was remembered with a monument on its former site.

In 1936 the Union Pacific Railroad sought to bring more travelers west by establishing one of the first complete winter resorts in the U.S. Sun Valley is still a premiere location for winter sports, as well as for year-round fun.

During World War II, Farragut Park became one of the country's major naval training centers.

In 1949 the National Reactor Testing Station was opened on an atomic reservation west of Idaho Falls. By 1951 it produced the first usable electricity ever generated by atomic power, and Arco became the first city to be lighted by atomic electricity.

Fifteen thousand Boy Scouts from all over the free world gathered at Farragut Park in August, 1967, for the first such gathering ever held in the U.S.

In 1975 Lewiston became an inland port, one of the nation's most distant from the sea. The Snake River Navigation Project placed the city at the head of 469 miles of Columbia-Snake river shipping.

The collapse of the Teton Dam in 1976 brought more than a billion dollars damage and wiped out much of the cattle industry of the state.

Another disaster, more distant, the eruption of Mt. St. Helens in Washington, in 1980, brought tons of ash to faraway portions of Idaho. Instead of disaster, in the Palouse area the next year's crops increased 30 percent.

Not so happy was the infestation of millions of grasshoppers in 1985, adding misery to the financially strapped farmers and costing the federal government 12 million dollars to spray 6,000,000 acres.

PERSONALITIES

If the federal government had kept its treaty with Chief Joseph of the Nez Perce Indians, they probably would have remained a peaceful and prosperous part of the three-state area including western Idaho. As it was, it became the sad duty of his younger son Joseph to lead his people on one of the longest and most difficult journeys in history. The military skill and statesmanship of Joseph the Younger certainly gives him an outstanding place in the imposing list of American Indian leaders. Moreover, many historians believe he deserves a place among the most notable leaders of the country.

On the long, bitter march, constantly pursued by federal troops, Joseph was masterful in avoiding conflict and in leading his cold and hungry people without destroying the areas through which they passed. At the bitter end, losing the last battle in far-off Montana, Joseph remained a noble loser.

Chief Tendoy of the Shoshone led a mixed group called the Lemhi tribe. He was helpful to early settlers and remained a friend of the Americans. For 25 years his statesmanship held off efforts to move his people to a reservation. It was only in 1909, two years after Tendoy's death, that they were forced to move.

One of the nation's best-known political leaders of his time was William Borah. He was the prosecutor at the famed trial of mine union leader William "Big Bill" Haywood. Famed attorney Clarence Darrow won the 1907 trial for the defense, but Borah had gained a national reputation for his part. At his death in 1940, Borah had served for 33 years in the U.S. Senate and had come to be called "one of the great statesmen of his time."

Borah was one of the leaders in the move to provide for direct election of the Senate by the people. He led the movement to reject the League of Nations but was prominent in other disarmament moves. As Chairman of the Senate Foreign Relations Committee for 16 years, he was a leader in the country's foreign policy. He strongly opposed U.S. entry into World War II but died just

PEOPLES

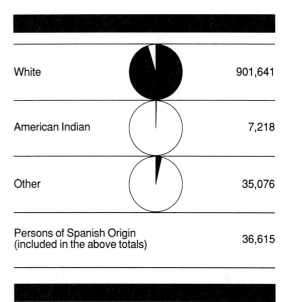

White	901,641
American Indian	7,218
Other	35,076
Persons of Spanish Origin (included in the above totals)	36,615

before that happened.

Another Idaho statesman, Frank Church of Boise, entered the U.S. Senate in 1957. In 1979 he, too, became Chairman of the Senate Committee on Foreign Relations.

The tragic death of world-renowned Ernest Hemingway at Ketchum on July 2, 1961, sent shock waves around the literary world. His personal tragedy served to emphasize one of the main themes of his writing—the destruction of personality and qualities of integrity that he felt had overwhelmed society as a result of two world wars.

In 1954 Hemingway won the Nobel Prize for literature.

THAT'S CURIOUS:
If Hemingway had lived, he might have been fascinated by the story of the man who robbed the bank of Troy, Idaho. When he got out of jail, he went to the same bank and asked for a car loan. The president gave him the loan and said he had paid his debt to society.

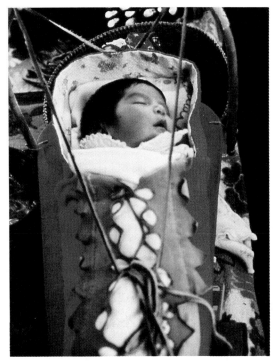

Indian baby in traditional finery, at Spalding

A WEALTH OF NATURE

Idaho still boasts many of the larger animals that were described by Lewis and Clark.

The variety of birds takes on the unexpected when, far from the ocean, shore and wading birds, pelican colonies and white egrets may be found, along with terns and sea swallows.

Of the more local bird varieties, the phalarope is one of the most unusual. The female has the bright colors, is dominant in the courtship and leaves the male to take care of the eggs.

One of the many previously unknown creatures discovered and noted by Lewis and Clark was the Idaho ring-necked scaup, a kind of duck, as well as the now rare Lewis bird and Clark's nutcracker.

The flight and call of the magnificent trumpeter swan provide nature lovers with one of the rare treats of the outdoors.

Close to 15 million trout are hooked in Idaho waters, with the Moyie River and Pend Oreille Lake said to be the finest fishing sources of their type.

Idaho can count more than 5 percent of the nation's commercial timber, including the world's largest stands of white pine. Some of the patriarchal red cedars may have reached 3,000 years of age.

Lewis and Clark were the discoverers of Idaho's state flower, the syringa. In blooming season in certain areas the syringa blossoms continue for unbroken miles.

Many of the root plants were so prized by the Indians that they often fought to claim the meadows where such plants as the valued camas grew and flourished.

Idaho possesses the world's largest reserves of phosphates, a total of a third of the mineral found on the continent.

Silver, gold, zinc, lead and copper have all had a leading place in the state's mineral resources. A wide variety of other valuable minerals may still be found. They include the variety of gemstones which give the state one of its nicknames—The Gem State.

The flow of Idaho streams and the groundwater provide an abundance of this most precious of all minerals. Much of the surface water used in irrigation returns through the soil to add to the huge underground water supplies.

USING THE WEALTH

Food processing is one of the state's leading industries. Two-thirds of all the processed potatoes produced in the U.S. come from Idaho, in the widest variety of products including potato flour.

Large-scale construction, energy research and testing, mobile homes and timber processing are all important in the economy.

Idaho leads all the states in silver production. The Sunshine Mine is said to be the largest silver producer in the U.S. The state is second in lead and zinc. Much of the supply of those three metals is processed from the same ore by different methods. The Sunshine Mine stands alone as a U.S. producer of antimony, another by-product of its operations.

Idaho continues to rank third in U.S. phosphate production.

When people ask to associate the word "potato" with another word, the word "Idaho" comes most often to mind. The potato is no longer the state's largest crop; today wheat ranks first as a crop, but cattle production brings in the largest share of agricultural revenue, surpassing all the field crops.

Despite its loss of first place, the Idaho potato is still claimed by many to be the best in the world. Idaho Falls is the center of the potato-producing region.

Moscow claims to be the dried pea and lentil capital of the U.S., producing nearly 100 percent of the country's supplies of those members of the bean family.

In 1975 Lewiston became the latest U.S. port, providing landlocked Idaho with a direct outlet to the sea. This

THE ECONOMY

in millions of $

Manufacturing	5,005
Agriculture	2,016
Service	1,200
Tourism	1,008
Mining	424

Principal Products:
lumber, food, chemicals

Agriculture:
cattle, wheat, dairy products, potatoes

marked the completion of the improvement of the tremendous Snake-Columbia waterway. However, steamboats had begun to puff their way up to Lewiston as early as 1861.

Pocatello is a major hub of both rail and air transport.

Highway building in the state has been difficult. It was not until 1962 that Highway 95 was opened to link north and south directly for the first time. The road was named for Lewis and Clark, who first blazed the trail it follows.

One of the great resources of the future will probably revolve around the development of Idaho's enormous hydroelectric power potential. Only about a fourth of this is currently in use.

GETTING AROUND

The story is told of a New York native who was sent to Idaho to work at an atomic installation. He came west

51

The thrills of Salmon River rafting

with great reluctance but soon was heard to remark, "Who wouldn't want to live here? Good climate, healthy air, honest people who are friendly, hunting and fishing, and other attractions on every side!"

Such widely different attractions as Hell's Canyon and Craters of the Moon attract hosts of visitors.

One of the awe-inspiring experiences of the continent is that of the visitor who stands at the bottom of Hell's Canyon, looking up for more than a mile and a half to the highest rim.

The canyon region remains much the same as it was before civilization came to Idaho. Pack trips into the wild provide the thrill of a lifetime for the tenderfoot.

One of the most publicized raft trips of all time was made by President Carter and his party in 1978. The trip empha-

sized again the popularity of one of the most exciting white water trips any-where—the spine-tingling ride down the River of No Return, the mighty Salmon.

Lewiston is the anchor of northern Idaho. Here the Snake and Clearwater rivers join to form one of the most striking settings for a town.

Spalding is home of the only national preserve of its kind, 22 scattered parcels of land which include many historic associations with the Nez Perce, Lewis and Clark and the early missionaries. This is Nez Perce National Historical Park.

One of the west's leading centers of culture and education is the Moscow area, home of the University of Idaho. It shares its fine symphony and other arts activities with nearby Pullman, Washington, another leading university town.

The Old Mission of the Sacred Heart near Cataldo is the oldest building in Idaho; it was constructed without nails.

In a land of beautiful lakes it is hard to pick the finest, but many experts have ranked Lake Coeur d'Alene as one of the world's most beautiful. The deep-blue waters change markedly with the varying conditions along their 30-mile stretch. Idaho's largest lake, Pend Oreille, is so large that heavy winds sometimes stir up 30-foot waves.

The cities of Coeur d'Alene and Sandpoint are important northern centers.

Many an Idaho area has ghost towns, and they provide visitors with unusual attractions. At one time Idaho City was almost as large as Boise. Only 28 of the 200 people buried in its cemetery died of natural causes. Silver City, perhaps the state's most noted ghost town, once rivalled any town in the state, but now only the spectators remain.

South-central Idaho has widely diverse attractions. Sun Valley is a leading resort, and Craters of the Moon National Monument is one of the most unusual areas on earth. No two of the fantastic shapes are alike—twists of rope, gloomy cones, natural bridges, hollow tubes of lava, craters—a million twisted forms.

Another unequalled spectacle was Thousand Springs, where each of the thousand outlets spurts from the cliffside. However, much of the time the water is siphoned off for power. Another natural feature is one of the largest and best known of all the balanced rocks, with a mighty shape perched on a tiny pedestal. Near Shoshone are the famous Indian Ice Caves.

American Falls was once a campsite for travelers on the Oregon Trail. Nearby Pocatello takes its name from friendly Chief Pokatello. It features a reproduction of old Fort Hall, Idaho State University, a fine art museum and historical museum.

Boise is not only the state capital but also is the largest Idaho city, home of much of the state's industry. One of its more unusual claims to fame is the use of natural hot water to heat many of the buildings. The Delamar house was the first in the nation to make such use of natural hot-spring water.

The imposing capitol was begun in 1905 and finished 15 years later. Idaho sandstone on the outside contrasts with Alaska marble on the interior. Pioneer self-taught artist Charles Ostner carved the statue of George Washington, now covered with gold leaf and dominating its location in the capitol. The pioneer artist gained fame in other media as well.

Among the cultural achievements of Boise was its founding in 1919 of National Music Week. Another annual event is the Basque Festival. The descendants of the Spanish shepherds are honored in this celebration which features Basque Oinkari dancers. A major social event is the Christmas Basque Sheepherders Ball.

COMPAC-FACS
IDAHO
Gem State—Spud State—Panhandle State
HISTORY
Statehood: July 3, 1890
Admitted as: 43rd state
Capital: Boise, founded 1863
OFFICIAL SYMBOLS
Motto: Esto Perpetua (May You Last Forever)
Animal: Appaloosa horse
Bird: Mountain bluebird
Flower: Syringa
Tree: White pine
Gem: Star garnet

The capitol

Song: "Here We Have Idaho"
GEO-FACS
Area: 83,564 sq. mi.
Rank in Area: 13th
Length (n/s): 490 mi.
Width (e/w): 305 mi.
Geographic Center: Custer, sw of Challis
Highest Point: 12,662 ft. (Borah Peak)
Lowest Point: 710 ft. (Snake River)
Mean Elevation: 5,000 ft.
Temperature, Extreme Range: 152 degrees
Number of Counties: 44 (plus small section of
Yellowstone Park)
POPULATION
Total: 1,001,000 (1984)
Rank: 40th
Density: 12.1 persons per sq. mi.

Principal Cities: Boise, 102,160; Pocatello,
46,340; Idaho Falls, 39,590; Lewiston, 27,986;
Twin Falls, 26,209; Nampa, 25,112; Coeur
d'Alene, 20,054
EDUCATION
Schools: 569 elementary and secondary
Higher: 9
VITAL STATISTICS
Births (1980/83): 64,000
Deaths (1980/83): 24,000
Hospitals: 52
Drinking Age: 19
INTERESTING PEOPLE
Joseph (elder, chief), Joseph (younger, chief),
Tendoy (chief), William E. Borah, Frank Church,
Ernest Hemingway, Sacajawea, David Thompson
WHEN DID IT HAPPEN?
1805: Lewis and Clark explore
1809: David Thompson builds Kullyspell House
1810: Fort Henry founded
1811: Wilson Price Hunt party passes through
1819: First fur trading rendezvous
1834: Wyeth builds Fort Hall
1836: Lapwai Mission established by Spaldings
1842: Father De Smet founds Sacred Heart
Mission
1846: Sacred Heart Mission moved to Cataldo
1860: Franklin, first permanent settlement; gold
strike
1862: Gold rush at Boise Basin
1863: Idaho Territory; Boise settled
1877: Nez Perce War
1878: Bannock War
1879: Sheepeater War
1890: Statehood
1899: Miners strike
1907: Steunenberg murder case
1924: Craters of Moon made national monument
1936: Sun Valley resort established
1951: First practical nuclear power generated
1967: World Jamboree of Boy Scouts
1975: Lewiston becomes port
1976: Teton Dam disaster
1985: Grasshopper infestation

THAT'S CURIOUS:
The vast wheat farms of the Palouse region climb over such steep hills that the combines which harvest the grain have to be self-levelling in order not to topple over on the rugged slopes.

MONTANA

FASCINATING MONTANA

Visitors today have no need to cure boredom the way the early Montana sheepherders used to do. There is plenty to see and do in the Land of the Shining Mountains.

Today's visitors can walk down a gulch that became the main street of a capital or visit the home of a one-time cowboy whose artistry in a single picture now would bring enough to buy the ranch where he once worked as a lowly hand.

They can stroll around the "richest hill on earth" or dig for beautiful gems in gooey clay, gaze at grasshoppers frozen perhaps millions of years ago, or visit the desolate field of a famous battle in which the only survivor of the losing side was a frightened horse.

The natural history of Montana tells of its uniquely divided geography, of the lake formed by an earthquake and of the family life of dinosaurs.

The history of the state recounts both dramatic events and interesting side-lights, such as the story of the ambitious man who employed 32 lawyers and was involved in as many as 40 lawsuits at one time.

There were the imaginary railroad towns, the houses that appeared to be mounds of wildflowers, the techniques used by the Indians to buffalo the buffalo, and the case of the disappearing governor.

Another, and more important mystery, was concerned with how the Indians obtained the repeating rifles which helped win the most talked-about Indian battle.

All these, the big and the little, the important and the intriguing, combine to make up the fascinating story of Montana.

THE FACE OF MONTANA

With 50 mountain ranges Montana ("mountain" in Spanish) certainly lives up to its name. The various ranges of the Rockies spread across the entire western fourth of the state. They reach their highest point in Montana at Granite Peak, just north of the Wyoming border.

The ragged border with Idaho follows the heights of the Bitterroot Range from its origin in the north to its southern end, then continues along the twists and turns of the Centennial Mountains until it reaches the western edge of Yellowstone Park and the Wyoming border a few miles farther east.

Montana is the only state where rainfall flows to Hudson Bay on the north, to the Pacific on the west and to the Gulf of Mexico on the south.

The Continental Divide that separates the waters of the east and west runs the entire width of the state from north to south. At Triple Divide Peak, that divide meets the divide which separates the rivers of the north from the rivers to the south. Lake Sherburne, St. Mary's Lake and Lake McDonald lie close together in Glacier National Park, but their waters flow in three different directions.

Three rivers join together at Three Forks to form the mighty Missouri River. Contrary to expectations, the Missouri

begins by flowing toward the northwest, then flows northeast and then almost directly east until it leaves Montana. The major tributary of the Missouri in Montana is the Yellowstone; it flows most of its length in the state but begins in Wyoming and enters the Missouri just east of the Montana border with North Dakota. South Dakota is the other neighboring state, and the northern border is the longest of all the states with Canada.

From the north, the Missouri's most important tributary is the Milk River, which begins in Glacier National Park, flows through Canada, re-enters the U.S. and meets the Missouri just east of Fort Peck Reservoir.

The major river flowing to the Pacific from Montana is the Clark Fork.

Fort Peck Reservoir is the largest lake in Montana. Like most of the other major lakes, it is manmade, formed behind Fort Peck Dam, once the largest earthen dam in the world. On the map, Flathead Lake would appear to be artificial, but it is the largest natural lake in Montana and one of the largest freshwater lakes east of the Mississippi.

Glacier National Park boasts more than 200 clear glacial lakes. The largest, Lake McDonald, is nearly 500 feet deep. Most of the thousands of smaller natural lakes are in the mountain areas.

The state's waters include many springs. Giant Springs near Great Falls is the largest of them.

In prehistoric times giant forces beneath the earth pushed up the mountains. The mountain-building force known as the Lewis Overthrust moved

present Glacier Park upward and eastward for 25 miles, leaving it in its present location.

The Beartooth Range began to rise "only" about 73 million years ago, then had a later uplift a mere million years in the past.

Other ancient underground forces at work in Montana included the many volcanoes which left their cones, lava sheets and volcanic ash.

All four of the great glaciers of the past covered much of the eastern section of the present state. The 50 glaciers now in Glacier National Park were not formed from the giant glaciers of the Ice Age. At the present rate of thaw, the present glaciers may someday disappear.

Montana is one of the richest sources of the remains of extinct creatures which once roamed there, including one of the most complete skeletons of the tyranosaurus rex dinosaur, as well as a nearly complete skeleton of the triceratops with three-foot horns over each of its eyes. Skeletons of 15-foot relatives of the horned toad were found near Billings.

People outside Montana who listen to weather reports hear of the bitter cold of winter there. There are extreme low temperatures, but winter cold is often broken by warm winds known as the Chinook. During one of them, the temperature may rise an amazing 70 degrees, and people will go about in shirtsleeves.

Western Montana is somewhat protected from the worst cold by the mountains, but the west gets much more snow.

EARLY DWELLERS

The earliest known peoples in Mon-

Opposite, Great Falls

tana were the Ancient Hunters, roaming the land perhaps as long ago as 12,000 years. They stalked the big-game animals with spear-pointed throwing sticks called atlatls.

In a hot and dry period on the plains, the people of the Middle Period no longer found the larger animals. They hunted the smaller game such as rabbits; the women dug up edible roots to add to the diet.

The Late Period ended only about a thousand years ago. People of that period found plenty of buffalo, which they killed by driving them over high ledges where they fell to their death.

After the Europeans began to explore in the south, an animal even more useful than the buffalo came into Indian life. Many European explorers' horses strayed or were stolen by the Indians. They multiplied until most of the tribes of the west not only owned horses but also had become skilled horsemen. The horse changed travel, warfare and many other aspects of Indian life.

The various groups of Crow and Blackfeet formed the largest population of the plains. Shoshone, Flathead, Arapaho, Cheyenne and Assiniboin also were found in the area.

For the most part the Indians made permanent lodges of mud on pole frameworks. Although the tepee was a permanent home to some, it was more generally used during travel.

The Indians continued to hunt buffalo as their prehistoric predecessors had done. Sometimes, an Indian would wear a buffalo head and robe to decoy the buffalo over a cliff, pursued by other hunters on horseback.

No part of a buffalo was wasted. The skin became blankets and clothing; horns and bones became utensils and the meat could be either eaten at once or made into a popular food known as pemmican. To make this dried meat, a kind of sausage, the buffalo meat was ground up, combined with berries and cured. It kept for a long time.

The Blackfeet were perhaps the most widely roaming of all the tribes, and they had many divisions. The Minnetaree Blackfeet were also known as the Gros Ventres of the River, and the Atsina were the Gros Ventres of the Mountains.

A small tribe known as the Sheepeater were found mostly in the Yellowstone region. They sometimes were called the Arrowmakers because of the beautiful arrowheads they chipped from the volcanic glass known as obsidian.

STIRRINGS

In 1742 the brothers Louis and Francis Verendrye were the first Europeans known to have visited present Montana.

James Mackay found and named the Yellowstone River in 1795, and other Europeans must have visited, but little was generally known about the area.

That soon changed after the U.S. made its Louisiana Purchase, which included all of Montana up to the great divide.

The explorers best known to present Americans, Lewis and Clark, were sent to

THAT'S CURIOUS:
Indians considered that stealing a horse was one of the best means of demonstrating a man's bravery, and it was not considered "wrong" by the Indians.

58

"Fort Union on the Missouri," by Carl Bodmer

gain information about the new possessions. On April 26, 1805, the explorers entered present Montana on the Missouri River near the mouth of the Yellowstone River. The Great Falls of the Missouri forced them to spend a month in portaging around the roaring waters.

When the explorers reached the three forks, Lewis concluded that "...those three forks are nearly of a Size...," that is, neither of the three was the main Missouri. He decided that the true Missouri River began at that junction, and later geographers agreed. The explorers named the three headwater rivers Jefferson, Madison and Gallatin.

The party became the first Americans to record a crossing of the Continental Divide, at present Lemhi pass. They had to trade with the Indians for horses to continue their journey across the continent. On their return trip in June, 1806, the party divided to explore further areas. Lewis' group found the upper Yellowstone near Livingston, and they floated down that river on Indian bull boats. The two parties reunited and returned to their base in St. Louis.

Upon hearing the accounts of Lewis and Clark, Manuel Lisa expanded his fur trading operations in 1807 by setting up the first trading station in Montana, where the Bighorn River joins the Yellowstone. The trading company of

THAT'S CURIOUS:

The Verendrey brothers were struck by the beauty of what they called the "shining mountains." Montana is still known as the Land of the Shining Mountains.

John Jacob Astor, the American Fur Company, set up a chain of forts in Montana to protect and accommodate the fur business.

With the virtual extinction of the beaver, the fur business ended, but the mountain men such as Jim Bridger, Hugh Glass and John Colter continued in the area and became famous for their many adventures.

As western migration brought thousands across the country, most passed south of present Montana. However, the trails provided little fodder for oxen and cattle. Dying strays were abandoned by their original owners and taken into Montana by Montana wranglers, where they were brought back to health on the wonderful grasses there. This gave a healthy start to the livestock industry.

EARLY GROWTH

In 1841 St. Mary's Mission was founded by Father Pierre Jean De Smet. Nearby Stevensville was founded and became the first permanent settlement in Montana.

Beginning in 1832, steamboats had been able to travel up the Missouri as far as Fort Union, which was built in 1842. In 1858 John Mullan pioneered the first road across the northern Rockies, which eventually reached 624 miles, from Fort Benton to Walla Walla, Washington.

In 1862 gold was discovered at Bannock, and almost overnight Montana's first town had a population of 500.

In 1863 a group of miners led by Bill Fairweather discovered gold at what they called Alder Gulch. Within a year, more than 10,000 people had swarmed into the community they named Virginia City.

With such an influx of population, Montana Territory was created on May 26, 1864.

In 1864 another gold discovery was made at Last Chance Gulch, now the main street of Helena. Another 1864 gold camp became the town of Butte.

One of the country's strangest political mysteries occurred when territorial Governor Thomas Francis Meagher boarded a steamboat at Fort Benton, went to his stateroom and was never seen again.

Eastern Montana had been set aside for the Indians by treaty, but settlers kept coming in illegally. When the treaty was scrapped and the government attempted to put the Indians on reservations, widespread war broke out.

Of course, the most remembered battle of this war took place in Montana in 1876, when George Armstrong Custer's force was defeated and wiped out on the banks of the Little Bighorn River. Another force under Major Marcus Reno survived after heavy fighting. Custer's handling of the battle still causes arguments among war experts. Among the unanswered questions is the source of the Indian's Winchester rifles, far superior to the guns of the Custer forces.

THAT'S CURIOUS:

In the spring many a stranger traveling in Montana would approach a mound of blooming wildflowers on the prairie only to be surprised to find the mound was a settler's home. In many places sod was the only available building material, and spring bloom would burst all over the houses.

Although medicine man Sitting Bull is often credited with the victory, he was not at the battle, but he apparently had accurate reports from his warriors. He theorized that the defeat was due to the great fatigue of Custer and his men, as well as to the superiority of the Indian weapons.

Another Indian leader, Chief Joseph, had led his people away from their western homeland to try to find amnesty in Canada. After a 1,600-mile retreat with all their belongings, they arrived in Montana in August, 1877. Joseph and his warriors were defeated at the Battle of Bear's Paw.

Settlers continued to come in, and irrigation started in 1882. Ever larger cattle herds were grazed. The horrible winter of 1886 wiped out many of the ranchers but the settlers made a comeback, and by 1889 Montana's growth finally brought about statehood.

UP-TO-DATE

President Theodore Roosevelt visited Gardiner in 1903 to dedicate the northern gateway to Yellowstone National Park.

The state made headlines in another way in 1916 when Jeannette Rankin became the first woman ever elected to the U.S. House of Representatives. She gained further attention when she voted against U.S. entry into World War I.

In 1922-23 other Montana members of Congress, Senators Burton K. Wheeler and Thomas J. Walsh, gained fame by

PEOPLES

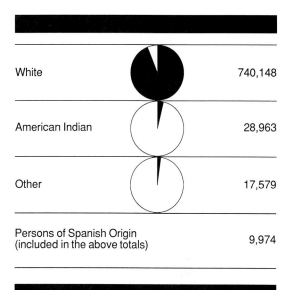

White	740,148
American Indian	28,963
Other	17,579
Persons of Spanish Origin (included in the above totals)	9,974

uncovering the scandal about oil leases at Teapot Dome. The Teapot Dome scandal rocked the Harding administration.

In 1932 Glacier National Park was rededicated as the U.S. section of the International Peace Park with Canada. The 1930's also saw severe earthquakes, drought and dust storms in Montana. Added to these troubles, the great depression forced most of Butte's mines to close. But prosperity eventually returned.

The earthquake of 1959 was one of the worst, even creating a new lake with the appropriate name of Quake Lake.

Great Falls became the headquarters of a great intercontinental ballistics missile complex in 1963, and the next

THAT'S CURIOUS:
Four brothers were born in the same house near Frenchtown, but each one was born in a different territory. Before it became a territory in its own right, Montana had been a part of five other territories.

year the state celebrated 75 years of statehood.

The year 1972 found the state replacing the constitution in use since 1889.

A startling discovery was made in 1978, when a dinosaur nest and eggs were uncovered near Choteau. This first such discovery in the Western Hemisphere indicates that some dinosaurs cared for their young.

In 1983 mining operations ceased in Butte, and the "richest hill on earth" became quiet, leaving thousands without jobs.

In 1985 the 75th anniversary of Glacier National Park was celebrated.

PERSONALITIES

Artist Charles M. "Charley" Russell was not born in the west, but he moved there as a boy. Based on his experiences as trapper, hunter, cowboy and sheepherder, Russell began to paint scenes of life on the open countryside. He became so skillful and so renowned as a painter-sculptor that Montana chose him as one of its representatives in the national Statuary Hall. Russell is the only artist to receive this honor.

Russell's first fame as an artist came in an unusual way. During the frightful winter of 1886, the absentee owner of the ranch where Russell worked wrote to ask about his herds. Russell painted a picture on an envelope of coyotes watching a starving range cow. He called it "Waiting for a Chinook (The Last of Five Thousand)." The foreman forwarded the picture to the owner, saying it told the story better than words; the painting became a popular subject for postcards.

In 1914 the artist's work was shown in London, and by his death at Great Falls in 1926 he had produced more than 4,500 watercolors, oils, sketches and bronze sculptures. His last unfinished work sold for $30,000, a huge sum at the time. Today, just one of his paintings might be worth as much as a ranch in Judith Basin where he started wrangling.

Russell has been recognized as one of the main sources of information about life in the west—an exciting and authentic depiction.

Frederic Remington came to Montana at the age of 13. He was another masterful painter of the horses, soldiers, cowboys and Indians of the west. His spirited action and sympathetic understanding of his subjects are notable in all his work.

In a shorter lifetime Remington completed more than half as many works as Russell. His 25 bronze sculptures are cherished in many museums and private collections.

His life experiences were broadened by service as a correspondent during the Spanish-American War. He wrote several books and did drawings for major magazines.

There is a Remington Art Museum at Ogdenburg, New York.

Although there were no survivors to describe the Custer massacre, artist Edgar S. Paxson spent years in research-

---

THAT'S CURIOUS:

Charley Russell overcame the loneliness and boredom of sheepherding in a constructive way by improving his art. Other sheepherders passed the time by piling rocks into high stacks called cairns. Some of them may still be seen.

"Custer's Last Stand," by Frederic Remington

ing all the known facts about the tragedy. His large panorama called "Custer's Last Stand" was completed after 23 years of study and work and is thought to be as authentic as possible under the circumstances.

Two Montana tycoons were friends early in their career but later engaged in a long bitter feud. Marcus Daly and William Andrews Clark each developed large fortunes in Montana. Daly bought the Anaconda claim and is known as the father of the Montana copper industry of the Butte area. Clark expanded his merchandising empire into banking and mining investments.

The two men took opposite sides and spent large sums in the fight for the Montana capital. Daly struggled to place the capital at Anaconda, and Clark worked for the winning Helena. Later, they were pitted against each other in the fight for the U.S. Senate. Clark was selected by the state legislature, but he was accused of bribery in the selection, and he could not take his seat. He tried four times and at last served a full term as senator. Daly died without having gained senatorial distinction.

Another determined mining man was Augustus Heinze. He was so anxious to control great mining interests that he kept as many as 32 lawyers active and at one time had 40 court actions on the dockets. He paid his miners to try to disrupt his competitors underground as well.

Mike Mansfield and Burton K. Wheeler both had outstanding service in the U.S. Senate.

Jeannette Rankin was a lifelong promoter of the cause of peace. She had the unusual record of voting against U.S. entry into both world wars, casting the only vote in Congress against World War II. As late as 1968, she led the Jeannette Rankin Brigade, a peace group protesting the Vietnam War. She also campaigned vigorously for women's causes.

Nobel Prize winner Harold C. Urey was a professor at the University of Montana. He captured the prize in 1934 for his work in chemistry.

One of the notable Indian women in American history was Sacajawea, who grew up near Three Forks. After she was captured by Minnetaree Indians, she was taken east by them and later married Tuissant Charboneau, a trapper. The couple were hired by Lewis and Clark as guides. The husband was not very effective, but Sacajawea was outstanding. She brought her infant son with her, and the boy practically became a junior member of the expedition.

Indian leader Robert Yellowtail became the first Indian ever to have a federal assignment to head a reservation.

Chief Plenty Coups was the last of the notable Crow leaders. He was selected to represent the Indian nations as a head of state at the dedication of the first unknown soldier's tomb at Arlington Cemetery.

A WEALTH OF NATURE

Montana has always been one of the richest states in mineral reserves. Despite the billions of dollars worth of minerals already extracted, there is said to be many billions more as yet untouched.

Billions of tons of coal reserves, oil and natural gas are still to be brought out.

Building stone, gem-quality corundum, and vermiculite are plentiful; gem sapphires of green aquamarine, cornflower and other colors are more numerous than those of any other state. Garnets, topaz, jasper and even an occasional diamond add to the rock hound's delight.

Meriwether Lewis described the wildlife he found as being extraordinary. Within a two-mile circle, he estimated that he saw 10,000 buffalo along with other animals large and small.

The explorers were terrified by the fury of the grizzly bears they encountered. "I had rather fight two Indians than one bear," Lewis wrote.

The buffalo and most of the grizzlies are gone from the wild, but Rocky Mountain goats (a kind of antelope), other antelope, bear, deer, moose and even bobcat may be found. The small number of rare white wolves found at Judith Basin were an interesting rarity.

Small animals are still captured for their fur.

THAT'S CURIOUS:
A wealthy cattleman sued a Chicago meat packer for failure to keep an agreement. When he went to court in Chicago, he brought a large group of his cowboys as witnesses. He sent them out on the town, saying, "Have a good time, boys...that company will pay for your entertainment." When the company lost, it paid for perhaps the largest group of witnesses ever involved in a trial.

Lewis and Clark first discovered many wild creatures, including the unique Maximillian jay.

More than 2,000 species of plants and flowers flourish in Montana, including vast numbers of the tiny alpine flowers of the lofty areas. The forest lands include those of eleven national forests.

USING THE WEALTH

Mineral wealth came first in Montana. Despite the fact that the 300 miles of mining tunnels under Butte are now closed, minerals still bring almost two billion dollars a year in revenue, coming mainly from petroleum, coal and natural gas.

Agriculture is not far behind minerals as a source of annual income, but manufacturing brings in almost twice as much income as minerals and agriculture combined. However, manufacturing is based mainly in the primary metals and petroleum. Lumber products are the third most important manufacturing resource. Libby has been called the Christmas tree capital of the United States.

In Montana agriculture, wheat is king, with Great Falls the center of the state's kingdom of wheat. Spring wheat is mostly grown by what is known as dry farming, without irrigation.

A small but glamorous industry is the mining and processing of the many kinds of sapphires found in the state. The gems are found in natural tubes of sticky clay. Separating the sapphires from the clay is a long and difficult process.

The refining of sugar beets, the milling of flour and lumber, and the manufacture of furniture are all important. Products needed in the mines and

THE ECONOMY

in millions of $

Manufacturing 4,290

Mining 1,732

Agriculture 1,503

Service 1,006

Tourism 423

Principal Products:
primary metals, lumber, petroleum

Agriculture:
wheat, cattle, barley, dairy products

on the farms and ranches range from mining machinery to fancy saddles.

A port is generally thought of as being on the seacoast, but far-off Montana in the heart of a continent has a port, perhaps the most remote from any ocean anywhere. The Missouri River was shallow and treacherous, but by 1859 steamboat building had reached a point where some of the steamboats "could float on a damp sponge" and so reach distant Montana.

From everywhere in the northern Rockies, passengers and goods flowed into Fort Benton, the farthest port reached by steamboats on the Missouri. Easing past the many dangerous sandbars and snags, the steamboats could carry the people and products of the distant north as far as the Gulf of Mexico.

Railroad tracks reached Montana

from both east and south in 1881. Two years later, tracks stretched clear across the state in spite of the difficulties of blasting long tunnels through mountains and other great construction problems.

GETTING AROUND

"Between the alpine splendor of Glacier National Park and the wonders of Yellowstone lies a land of breathtaking natural beauty," as one visitor exclaimed.

The gateways to these parks are particularly impressive. Three of the five entrances to Yellowstone are on the Montana side. Beartooth Highway, the northeast Yellowstone gateway, has been called one of the most scenic highways in the world. It passes by one of the country's truly unique sights, Grasshopper Glacier, where millions of grasshoppers were embedded in the glacial ice and may still be seen in layers which look almost solid black from a distance.

Another spectacular road is Going-to-the-Sun Highway, twisting over the Continental Divide and crossing magnificent Glacier National Park. Visitors who take to the many trails enjoy the primitive wilderness and glimpse the wildlife of the park, which includes about 200 grizzly bears, the Montana state animal. Just east of the park is the Museum of the Plains Indian in Browning. The National Bison Range is one of the oldest big-game preserves in the U.S.

North-central Montana is sometimes called Charlie Russell Country. The famed artist lived and worked at Great Falls, and his home and studio are preserved much as he left them. The nearby museum and gallery display some of his paintings and sculpture. Especially interesting is Russell's collection of authentic costumes used in his paintings.

In the northeast corner of the state, the mighty Missouri River sets the theme for the entire landscape. The Fort Peck Dam has turned the river into a great lake. Beyond the lake, visitors who follow the famed Lewis and Clark trail markers, which stretch for 1,940 miles across the state, will find many areas little changed from the time of the great explorers.

Visitors to the dreary prairie site of Custer Battlefield National Monument view with awe the locale of the most famous of all U.S. Indian battles. A simple marble column records the names of those who fell.

Near Pryor, Indian history is preserved in the home of Chief Plenty Coups, now a state monument. Another state monument, Pictograph Cave, south of Billings, preserves the remains of a prehistoric culture of 5,000 years ago.

Southwest Montana is known as Gold West Country, "where history resides in restored gold mining camps." No longer a ghost town because of its tourist boom, Virginia City recalls the memory of one of the west's most famous boom towns, including Boothill Cemetery, where outlaws came to final rest.

Much of Montana's history was written in mineral-rich Butte. Old architecture, historic mines, museums and

THAT'S CURIOUS:

There were no towns on the Central Montana Railroad, so the railroad president named several on the map. Two young ladies named Fan and Lulu were visiting his daughter; he named one of the imaginary towns Fanalulu.

monuments recall those colorful times.

Butte claims to perch on the richest hill on earth. Great wealth has come from the area, and the city believes that more is still to come.

The capital of Helena has grown into a modern city. It sprang up around Last Chance Gulch, now the main street. Its many curves were said to be designed so that gunfighters would not have a straight shot.

The classic dome of the state capitol has an appropriate sheathing of copper. A famed mural by Charles Russell shows the meeting of the Indians with Lewis and Clark at Ross Hole. This and other murals of the building make up one of the finest collections of its type.

Another striking building is St. Helena Cathedral, modeled after the cathedral of Cologne, Germany.

At the El Dorado Sapphire Mine northeast of Helena, visitors are welcome to try their luck digging for sapphires and other stones.

Nearby are the great bluffs cut by the Missouri River through the immense body of solid rock. Meriwether Lewis called them "the Gates of the Rocky Mountains."

Most Montanans would heartily agree.

COMPAC-FACS

MONTANA
Treasure State—Big Sky Country—Land of the Shining Mountains

HISTORY
Statehood: November 8, 1889
Admitted as: 41st state
Capital: Helena, settled 1864
OFFICIAL SYMBOLS
Motto: Oro y plata (Gold and silver)
Animal: Grizzly bear

Vacation fun at the Lone Mountain Guest Ranch

Bird: Western meadowlark
Fish: Blackspotted cutthroat trout
Flower: Bitterroot
Tree: Ponderosa pine
Grass: Bluebunch wheatgrass
Gem Stones: Agate and sapphire
Song: "Montana" (music by J.E. Howard, lyrics by C.C. Cohan)
GEO-FACS
Area: 147,046 sq. mi.
Rank in Area: 4th
Length (n/s): 315 mi.
Width (e/w): 580 mi.
Geographic Center: In Fergus Co., 12 mi. w of Lewistown
Highest Point: 12,799 ft. (Granite Peak)
Lowest Point: 1,800 ft. (Kootenai River)
Mean Elevation: 3,400 ft.
Temperature, Extreme Range: 187 degrees
Number of Counties: 56 (plus small areas of Yellowstone Park)
POPULATION
Total: 824,000 (1984)
Rank: 44th
Density: 6 persons per sq. mi.

The capitol

Principal Cities: Billings, 66,824; Great Falls, 56,725; Butte-Silver Bow, 37,205; Missoula, 33,388; Helena, 23,938; Bozeman, 21,645; Havre, 10,891

EDUCATION
Schools: 292 elementary and secondary
Higher: 8

VITAL STATISTICS
Births (1980/83): 47,000
Deaths (1980/83): 22,000
Hospitals: 67
Drinking Age: 19

INTERESTING PEOPLE
Meriwether Lewis, William Clark, Charles M. (Charley) Russell, Frederic Remington, Marcus Daly, William Andrews Clark, Augustus Heinze, Mike Mansfield, Burton K. Wheeler, Gary Cooper, Chet Huntley, Jeannette Rankin, Myrna Loy, Brent Musberger, Harold C. Urey, Sacajawea, Chief Plenty Coups , Pierre Jean De Smet

WHEN DID IT HAPPEN?
1743: Verendrey brothers explore
1795: Naming of Yellowstone River
1805: Lewis and Clark explore
1806: Lewis and Clark return
1807: Manuel Lisa sets up first trading post
1841: St. Mary's Mission founded by De Smet
1859: Steamboat first reaches Fort Benton
1862: Gold discovery at Bannack
1863: Alder Gulch bonanza, Virginia city begins
1864: Montana Territory established, Helena founded
1876: Custer massacred
1880: Railroad spans state
1895: Montana State University begins classes
1909: National Bison Range created
1915: Elk Basin petroleumn discovery site
1926: Charles M. Russell's death
1938: Going-to-the-Sun Highway finished
1959: Severe earthquake damage in southeast
1964: Territorial centennial
1972: New constitution
1983: Butte mining operations cease
1985: 75th anniversary of Glacier as National Park

THAT'S CURIOUS:

When General Terry reached the site of the Custer battle, he found only desolation. Of all the men and animals of Custer's force, only the horse Comanche remained, neighing forelornly and stamping his foot.

NEVADA

FASCINATING NEVADA

Did an ancient race of giants wear the giant moccasin? What was the meaning of the important toothmark? How did a wilderness area become the "second city of the west" in less than four years? How did a second-hand bag of flour bring in $275,000 for charity? Whose fault was the "biggest?" How did a drunk manage to name a town? The story of Nevada is filled with such fascinating questions (and answers).

The skiing mailman, the man who received President Lincoln's last communication, the couple that built a great mansion in the wilderness and then lost everything they had. These are just a few of the colorful characters whose lives unfold in the annals of Nevada.

Nevada history tells of the horses with multicolored polka dots, of the only state constitution ever transmitted in its entirety by telegram (at great cost), of the lost city, of the wealth that saved the Union, of the waste clay that turned into fortunes in silver and of the ancient duck decoys.

Nevada is the state of such contrasts as the smallest state capital in the country and the world's major gambling and entertainment center—all part of a great empire forged from desert lands in scarcely more than a lifetime.

THE FACE OF NEVADA

"There are miles and miles of Nevada where nothing moves but you and wildlife," according to the Nevada Commission on Tourism. More than 75 percent of the state's population lives in the regions of Las Vegas and Reno.

Outside those areas, cattle and sheep ranches in the north and central sections and irrigated valleys support most of the population. The rest of this immense state sees few people in a land of sand, rocks and sagebrush. The key to population is water, and Nevada is the driest of all the states. This is due to the great "wall" that keeps most of the rain away—the tremendous curtain of the Sierra Nevada Mountains catching the moisture before it can reach the Nevada side.

Running north and south across the state are other, smaller mountain chains.

The rivers of the far north drain into the Snake River; those to the south flow into the Colorado River. Most of the other rivers of Nevada go nowhere, ending in desolate alkali sinks, unless they have been diverted for irrigation. The Humboldt is the largest of these going-nowhere rivers. The coy Amargosa River flows most of its course underground. The Truckee River ends in Pyramid Lake, but that lake, largest wholly within Nevada, has no outlet. The Walker River ends in Walker Lake, but it too has no outlet. Beautiful Lake Tahoe, high in the Sierras, is shared with California.

Backed up behind Hoover Dam, the waters of the Colorado River have formed Lake Mead. Farther south, Lake Mohave also has backed up waters of the Colorado. That great river and its artificial lakes have transformed the desert, providing water for much of the southwest.

The section of the Colorado River below Hoover Dam forms the small natural boundary of Nevada with Arizona. The rest of the state's borders are manmade, including the imaginary line across Lake Tahoe that separates California and Nevada. Utah, Idaho and Oregon are the other border states.

In very ancient times, Nevada was covered with shallow seas. The land rose and fell several times; the forces beneath the earth finally raised the general level of the land, and erosion from the mountains brought more soil to add to the levels, until much of the state has become a huge plateau within the Great Basin.

Walker and Pyramid lakes are all that remain of enormous lakes that covered much of the state in more recent prehistoric times. Pyramid Lake is named for the craggy rock formations that rise from its surface in the form of rough pyramids. One of these pyramids has a hot spring which sends out clouds of steam, making it look like a miniature volcano.

Other parts of Nevada also have hot springs, but even more unusual is Beowawe Geyser Basin. After the Yellowstone geysers, this is the largest collection of geysers in the country.

Other underground forces, volcanoes, have covered much of the surface around extinct Lunar Crater with lava, including chunks the size of city blocks.

Opposite, Astronaut's-eye view of Las Vegas' famous "Strip"

EARLY DWELLERS

The mark of a single tooth has made it possible for archeologists to determine that people have lived in present Nevada for 23,800 years, probably much longer. This human toothmark on a bone was found near Tule Springs, and carbon dating gives a fairly precise reading of the age.

Thousands of relics of prehistoric occupation have been brought from Lovelock Caves. Well-preserved mummies have been found in Nevada caves. The dry climate has helped to preserve these relics in much the same way as those of ancient Egypt. Not generally found elsewhere is an unusual type of relic, the painted and feathered duck decoys crafted by ancient hunters.

As the generations went by, the people of the area began to grow crops, watered by well-designed irrigation systems; they mined salt, wove baskets and fashioned glazed and decorated pottery. They also wove cloth from cotton which they grew and spun. This was all accomplished in the period B.C.

Many of the objects left by the prehistoric peoples have been preserved and exhibited at the State Historical Museum at Reno.

The Pueblo people from the south moved into southern Utah to build one of their stone and adobe communities, now called Pueblo Grande. When this treasure disappeared under the waters of Lake Mead, it became known as the Lost City.

THAT'S CURIOUS:
Whose fault is it? In the case of Nevada the fault is "one of the most spectacular faults in the world." This fault is a line where the earth on one side of a great crack is settling faster than it is on the other. Sudden movements along such a line cause earthquakes.

Cathedral Gorge State Park

Despite the inhospitable nature of the region, by the time early European explorers reached the area, the Indian population was large, perhaps even larger than in similar areas in the east where living was much easier.

The majority of Nevada Indians belonged to the Shoshonean group. The various subgroups were the Shoshone, Utes, Goshutes and Paiutes. Around the Lake Tahoe region, the smaller group of Washoe (Wasau) made their home. Apparently, they had no relationship to their neighbors. They were especially skilled in basket making. One of the greatest weavers who ever lived was a member of this group.

The Indians worked the turquoise mines of the region and probably traded this valuable stone with the skilled jewelers of far-off Mexico.

STIRRINGS

During the 1770's several Spanish explorers approached and may have reached parts of present Nevada. However, the area had such a reputation for desolation that few Europeans ventured in.

Then, in 1827, Jedediah Smith crossed part of Nevada on his way to California. The next year, trader Peter Skene Ogden discovered the Humboldt River, and Joseph Walker traveled along that river on his way to California in 1833-34. The southern part of Nevada was crossed by the Old Spanish Trail in the late 1830's.

Guided by the extraordinary scout Kit Carson, John C. Fremont explored much of the region between 1843 and 1845. In 1846 Mexico gave up claim to the region after its war with the U.S.

The stage was set for the great rush of travelers hurrying across the barren lands to reach the gold of California, beginning in 1849. They came on foot, on mules, on horseback, in covered wagons. The last stretch across the 40 miles of alkali desert caused great hardship and death.

Formed in 1850, the Territory of Utah included Nevada. Almost as soon as the Mormons had settled in Utah, they came into Nevada to set up trading stations to serve the travelers. In 1851 they established Mormon Station, first permanent white settlement in what is now Nevada. As time went by, the Mormons established Pioche, Mottsville, Genoa and Big Meadows, now called Lovelock. By the end of 1851 Genoa was flourishing as the county seat of Carson County.

After gold was discovered in Gold Canyon, prospectors began to move up the canyon in search of the precious metal. They were greatly disturbed by the blue clay that stuck to the gold. Then, well-educated prospectors Hosea and Allen Grosch discovered that the clay was almost solid silver. Both brothers died soon afterwards without ever revealing their secret. However, H.T.P. Comstock knew they had made a rich strike, and he was determined to find it. He talked about the wealth of the area so much that eventually the whole area became known as the Comstock Lode. The silver riches were rediscovered in 1859, and silver became far more plentiful than gold.

Unsuccessful gold seekers hurried in from California, and almost overnight the undeveloped area was overwhelmed by a crowd that finally reached more than 25,000. A community called Virginia City grew up almost overnight.

The winter of 1859 was rough, with supplies giving out and prices skyrocketing until a bag of flour sold for eighty-five dollars. As soon as the first load of new flour got through, some of the prospectors were so hungry they mixed it with snow and ate it raw.

The valuable ores soon were flowing out of Virginia City on wagons, and those same wagons were bringing back food and other needed supplies and soon all the luxuries that wealth could buy, as well.

In an amazingly short time, the ore was being processed on the site by means of a method discovered by Almarin Paul, a local man.

Virginia City had become something of a wilderness metropolis by 1863. It continued to grow and flourish with lavish homes, fine churches, a striking courthouse and an opera house where almost every star of the day appeared—all built on the great fortunes that were made, and frequently lost, as well. After San Francisco, Virginia City had become the second city of the west.

While all this had been going on, the nation had gone to war. The wealth of Nevada was so important to the war effort that President Lincoln said, "...the gold and silver in the region...has made it possible for the government to maintain sufficient credit to continue this terrible war for the Union."

When President Lincoln proposed statehood for Nevada, the region that had been a wilderness only four years before became a state in 1864. President Lincoln managed to push this act through Congress because he needed the three extra votes that Nevada could provide in Congress to approve his constitutional amendment abolishing slavery.

To get the new state constitution to President Lincoln when he needed it, the entire document was sent by telegram from Virginia City. The $3,400 fee was the highest ever paid for a telegram up to that time.

To celebrate statehood, the Comstock people hauled a 40-foot flag with 35 stars to the top of the mountain, raised it with a huge 36th star on top. Born as a product of the Civil War, Nevada became the "Battle Born State."

UP-TO-DATE

The first two senators from Nevada, William Stewart and James Nye, and the single congressman did vote for the 13th Amendment, and Nevada was one of the early states to ratify it. President Lincoln said this amendment saved thousands of lives by shortening the war, as well as freeing the slaves.

Eureka, Hamilton and other communities had rich strikes of minerals, and the Comstock continued to add wealth, but by this time most of the Virginia City area mineral rights had been acquired by four Bonanza Kings—Flood, O'Brien, Fair and Mackay. They gained their wealth before the minerals began to fade. By the mid-1880's, Virginia City had became almost a ghost town.

The first twentieth-century strike was made by Jim Butler at Tonopah; although it did not compare with Comstock, Tonopah yielded more than 135 million dollars. Goldfield was another boom town of the period. Then it, too, faded into a ghost.

The prosperity that followed World War I was in turn followed by the great depression of the 1930's. To overcome the hard times, Nevada legalized gambling and made divorce easy. At that time, Reno and Las Vegas were small dusty towns. Reno was first to benefit from the new laws and soon became the country's divorce capital, with gambling an extra attraction during the short stay required for a divorce.

The building of Hoover Dam brought about the boom at Boulder City as workers were paid well to build the great structure, which was completed in 1936.

After World War II, Nevada was chosen for testing atomic weapons. Beginning in 1951, the Nevada Proving Ground of the Atomic Energy Commission was the principal testing site in the country.

During the 1970's, Nevada population

THAT'S CURIOUS:

James Fennimore, known as Old Virginny because he came from Virginia, fell down drunk one night and smashed a bottle of whiskey against a rock. Rather than waste the whiskey entirely, he called out, "I christen thee Virginia City." That is the story told about the naming of the town.

grew at a 20 percent rate. In the late 70's ranchers took part in the "Sagebrush Rebellion," a movement designed to diminish federal control of the land. Eighty-five percent of Nevada land is controlled by the national government.

The census of 1980 showed that Nevada had by far the largest percentage growth of population of all the states. During the previous decade, the population had increased by 63.8 percent, rising from a low-ranked 49th in population to 43rd among the states.

PERSONALITIES

One of the world's great artists was born in Nevada long before Europeans arrived. She lived in the state for nearly 100 years. This extraordinary woman has become almost completely forgotten.

Dat-So-La-Lee was a member of the Washoe tribe, the country's most skilled weavers. She learned all the secrets of their basket making and became the most accomplished of all.

Using natural materials which she gathered herself, and working with only her fingernails, teeth and some broken pieces of glass, she fashioned 256 of the most perfect baskets ever created.

There was no artificial coloring in her work. The black was the stem of the mountain fern, the red that of the redbud and so on with other materials. The shapes and patterns of her work were drawn from the traditions of her people.

PEOPLES

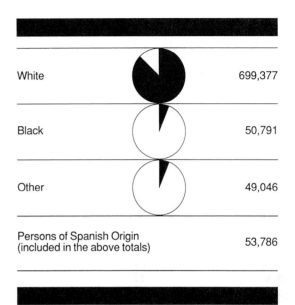

White	699,377
Black	50,791
Other	49,046
Persons of Spanish Origin (included in the above totals)	53,786

She illustrated their legends, myths and accomplishments in a way that no one else has achieved. Some of her baskets took a year to make.

In later life Dat-So-La-Lee lived with a Carson City couple during the winter, but she continued to live and work in the open at other times.

In her 96th year she was still working vigorously; when death came, she left an unfinished basket, which many buyers wanted to acquire. However, it was buried with her according to her tribe's custom.

Even during her lifetime, one of her baskets sold for the then unbelievable

THAT'S CURIOUS:

When Reuel Gridley of Austin lost an election bet, he had to carry a heavy sack of flour from his bakery around the town. To raise money for the war charities, he auctioned off the flour. The buyer gave the bag back to him; he went around the state auctioning off the flour and getting it back every time. Altogether, the flour bag raised $275,000 for the war Sanitary Fund. This was the first large-scale charity drive in the country.

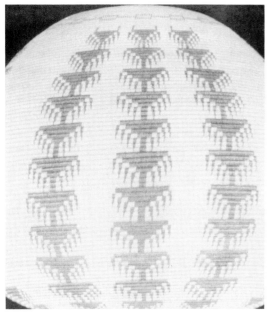

A basket woven by Dat-So-La-Lee

sum of $10,000. Now the world's greatest museums are proud to display her work. Some of the best is in the Smithsonian Institution at Washington, D.C.

Despite the general lack of knowledge about her life and work, some authorities have called her "one of the great artists of all time."

Samuel Clemens had saved some money from his work as a Mississippi River pilot. When his brother Orion Clemens was appointed Secretary of Nevada Territory in 1861, he borrowed from his brother, Sam, to make the trip, and Sam went along for the ride. Orion Clemens was an efficient beaurocrat. The territorial governor was away from Virginia City for long periods of time, and Orion Clemens practically ran the territory. When he left the post, he went into obscurity.

His brother, Samuel, of course, became the famous writer who took the name Mark Twain. Twain got his start in writing by working on the local newspaper. To add some spice to the dreary life of the mines, Twain kept his articles light and humorous, dreaming up many a witty story.

Even though he went on to world fame, Mark Twain said he looked back on his days in the rip-roaring mining town of Virginia City as among the happiest of his life.

He was able to meet all the famous people who flocked to Virginia City; he went on to the territorial legislature as a reporter, became acquainted with most of the lawmakers and gained his start as a writer there.

Eilley Orrum and Sandy Bowers both struck it rich on the Comstock. When they married, they agreed to have only the finest life. Their income might have reached 3 million a year. For the mansion they built, they imported Italian marbles, silver bathroom fixtures and every other luxury they could think of. They even piped in hot mineral water.

The handsome leatherbound books in their library were lost on Sandy, who could not read.

They went abroad and may even have been presented to the Queen of England, and they brought back fine art treasures. However, their luxury was not to last. The mines gave out; Sandy died at age 35. Eilley was cheated out of the balance of her fortune and died forgotten and in poverty.

George Hearst increased the fortune he had made in California by investing in the Comstock; when his Comstock wealth came in, he invested it wisely in such properties as a San Francisco newspaper. His son, William Randolph Hearst, continued the newspaper business founded by his father and became one of the wealthiest and best-known figures in America.

The "Big Four" of the Comstock managed to hang onto their money and make much more, but they invested their wealth outside the state. One of them, James Fair, did become a Nevada senator, but he used his fortune to restore San Francisco after the earthquake and fire.

Entirely different was the career of John Thompson. He is a kind of patron saint of skiers for having introduced the use of skis in America. On his skis he carried the mails over rough and dangerous routes for 20 years, and his grave at Genoa is marked by skis carved in stone.

James Nye was appointed by Lincoln as territorial governor. He became very popular with the people there. He was chosen as one of Nevada's original members of the U.S. Senate and gained fame for his oratory.

The other of Nevada's first two senators was William Morris Stewart. He made a fortune as a lawyer for the mining barons. His career flourished in Washington, and he was the author of the 15th Amendment, which assures all citizens the right to vote.

One of the great Indian friends of the settlers was Ute chief Old Winnemucca, who gave his name to the Nevada city.

A WEALTH OF NATURE

The mineral wealth of Nevada has not been exhausted by the mining of the past. The state is so vast that new strikes of gold and silver and other minerals are very possible. High-grade iron ore and coal are found, as well as copper. There may be extensive oil fields.

Surprisingly, perhaps, Nevada is the world's turquoise center, with more than 80 percent of all turquoise coming from Nevada mines. The world's largest turquoise chunk was found in the Battle Mountain area. It weighed 152 pounds.

Nevada also produced the largest black opal known at the time. The rare fire opal and other opals are found in the state.

Jasper, garnet, wonder stone, geodes, agates, quartz and beryl are among the gems that excite rock hounds.

Pyramid Lake has many surprises. In that far inland body of water is found the largest rookery of pelicans in the west, on Anaho Island in the lake. The lake also holds great landlocked salmon and the big Lahontan cutthroat trout. Lake Tahoe and Lake Mead are also popular for their fishing.

Bow and arrow hunting of deer is a popular sport, and stalking the state animal, rare bighorn sheep, with a camera is exciting. Unfortunately, the magnificent animal is seldom seen these days.

Although many sections of Nevada

THAT'S CURIOUS:

When Mark Twain offended a rival newspaperman at Virginia City, he was forced to agree to a duel with pistols. Twain was much relieved when the opponent refused to go through with it. However, when he heard he was about to be arrested for breaking a new law against dueling, Twain left Nevada for greener fields.

are barren and treeless, the higher areas are forest-covered and provide a variety of timber.

USING THE TREASURE

Nevada is the only state where tourist income and services for tourists provide the greatest sources of revenue.

Las Vegas calls itself the gaming and entertainment capital of the world. Lake Mead, Reno, Lake Tahoe, Virginia City and many attractive desert areas all hold the widest varieties of lures for tourists. Sportsmen can combine gambling, fine dining and top entertainment with some of the finest skiing, fishing and hunting.

One of the major contributions made by Nevada engineers and inventors was the development of new processes for milling and extracting minerals from hard rock and other difficult materials. The system of mine tunnel reinforcement called square sets was developed on the Comstock by Philip Deidesheimer and was adopted throughout the world. He is said to have devised this system by studying the construction of beehives.

Another contribution to mining engineering was made by Adolph Sutro, who devised a means of ridding mine tunnels of underground water.

Mercury, copper, gold and titanium are among the important mineral products of the state today.

It is not surprising that production of mining machinery, equipment and supplies are important in a mining state. Of course, processing of minerals also is still a leading industry. Cement production is

Hoover Dam

another important business.

Many large businesses have established headquarters or branches in Nevada. They have been encouraged to come in by laws designed to make the state attractive to business.

One of journalism's most interesting stories centers on the "Territorial Enterprise." The ability of Joseph Goodman and his staff of writers and editors, the exciting news they were reporting from Virginia City and the quality of their editorials soon made their newspaper an international success. Enterprise editorials were quoted worldwide. Performers who appeared at the opera house could be "made" or "broken" by the writing of an Enterprise critic. Many top artists refused to appear in Virginia City for fear of an unfavorable review.

Mark Twain was one of the early Enterprise journalists, and he gained his first fame as a writer there.

Completion of the continental railroad in 1869 greatly helped progress in Nevada. Mining towns were connected by short line road to the mainline. One of the most famous of these, Virginia and Truckee Railroad out of Virginia City, was known as the "richest shorthaul railroad in United States history."

Today, the international airport at Las Vegas has world importance, and the Reno-Tahoe region is served by many air connections.

One of the world's great construction projects was the building of Hoover Dam.

THE ECONOMY

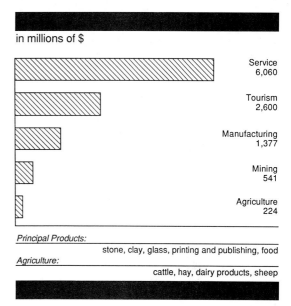

in millions of $

Service 6,060
Tourism 2,600
Manufacturing 1,377
Mining 541
Agriculture 224

Principal Products:
stone, clay, glass, printing and publishing, food
Agriculture:
cattle, hay, dairy products, sheep

This structure provides electricity and water resources for a vast radius of the southwest. Income from the water and electricity of the dam has been used to pay for its great cost.

As energy sources dwindled in the U.S., efforts were begun to tap the thermal energy of the Beowawe Geyser field. However, the efforts were plagued by failures, due mostly to the plugging of many of the natural vents to divert the steam to drilled wells. Nevertheless, Chevron continued to drill geothermal wells in the mid 1980's in hopes of operating a 16.6 Mw power plant south of the huge sinter terrace at Beowawe.

THAT'S CURIOUS:

Residents of Virginia City were amused by the white horses with multicolored polka dots. Their owner used the horses to crush the minerals, and the colors came from the chemicals he used in the process.

Fremont Street, Las Vegas

GETTING AROUND

"Dry, dusty ghost towns, electric cities that don't know day from night, cool, blue alpine lakes, meandering rivers soaked up by a thirsty desert—Nevada is a land of contrast that defies comparison," as one of the state's boosters sees it. "...there are places, things and events you just can't find anywhere else."

That is particularly true of one Nevada town which has to be unique in the world. Las Vegas is "the most exciting city ever built," according to its backers.

Most visitors come to Las Vegas for the excitement. The gambling palaces with their reeling slot machines, shuffling cards and rolling dice entice players around the clock. Is there a big-name entertainer who has not appeared in Vegas? Most residents would say "No," and many top stars return regularly to the Strip.

There is much more to Las Vegas than gambling, including the highest-paying rodeos, top-flight golf tournaments, classy auto races and championship boxing. Three different theme amusement parks also lure visitors. For history buffs there is the old Norman

THAT'S CURIOUS:
Senator William Stewart went to the White House to introduce a friend to President Lincoln. The President sent out a note saying that he had to go to the theater with Mrs. Lincoln and would see the two men in the morning. That was the evening of Lincoln's assassination, and the note is thought to be his last writing.

Fort and the Nevada State Museum and Historical Society.

Not far removed is Red Rock Canyon and the winter sports of Mt. Charleston.

Boulder City once housed the workers of Hoover Dam. Today the tidy city is the only place in Nevada where gambling is not allowed. The Visitor Center and tours are highlights of a visit to the dam. Lake Mead provides unparalleled fishing, swimming, diving and water skiing.

At Overton, the Lost City Museum demonstrates the Pueblo culture once thriving in the area.

North of Nevada's southern point is pioneer territory, where the Mormons first settled. Once the state's largest city, Goldfield is now a leftover of a rich past.

Northern Nevada has been called Covered Wagon Territory. Here the modern interstate follows the trail which brought so many hardships to the pioneers. Wendover is booming and growing with hotels and casinos at the edge of Bonneville Salt Flats. Each year, the town of Elko celebrates with its unique festival of the Basque, Spanish shepherds who settled in the area.

Since its days as a Truckee River crossing, Reno has billed itself as the "Biggest Little City in the World." Some of the best-known casinos rise above the colorful downtown arch, including one casino that calls itself the world's largest. Reno also has its share of entertainment spectaculars.

The Nevada Historical Society Museum, famous Harolds Club, advertised around the world, with its famed gun collection and Harrah's Auto Collection, world's largest, are all favorites with Reno visitors.

The University of Nevada, the Fleischmann Atmospherium-Planetarium and Mackay School of Mines Museum are other Reno attractions.

Tucked into the hills southeast of Reno lies Virginia City, center of the historic Comstock Lode. The entire town is a museum, a patchwork of tumbledown shacks, rich Victorian mansions, mine dumps and cemeteries.

High in the mountains, Lake Tahoe is on almost every list of the most beautiful bodies of water in the world. From quiet, unspoiled shores to the excitement of a huge casino, Tahoe satisfies almost every taste.

Smallest of all the state capitals, Carson City was born as a supply and shipping point for the rich mines of the silver strike. Housed in the old U.S. mint, the Nevada State Museum recalls those days with life-size displays of hard-rock mining. The Virginia-Truckee Railroad Museum and the governor's mansion, along with several stately Victorian homes, add to the interest of the city. The fine state capitol was completed in 1871 in only eight month's time. It often has been described as one of the most dignified and charming of all the capitols.

The name of the capital city pays tribute to the scout and explorer, Kit Carson.

THAT'S CURIOUS:

Boulder Dam is taller than a 70-story building. If all the materials it contains could be loaded into railroad flatcars, the train would reach all the way from Boulder City to Kansas City.

The capitol

COMPAC-FACS

NEVADA
The Silver State—Battle Born State—
Sagebrush State

HISTORY
Statehood: October 31, 1864
Admitted as: 36th state
Capital: Carson City, founded 1858
OFFICIAL SYMBOLS
Motto: All for Our Country
Animal: Desert bighorn sheep
Bird: Mountain bluebird
Flower: Sagebrush
Tree: Single-leaf pinon
Song: "Home Means Nevada"
GEO-FACS
Area: 110,561 sq. mi.

Rank in Area: 7th
Length (n/s): 483 mi.
Width (e/w): 329 mi.
Geographic Center: In Lander Co., 26 mi. se of Austin
Highest Point: 13,143 ft. (Boundary Peak)
Lowest Point: 470 ft. (Colorado River)
Mean Elevation: 5,500 ft.
Temperature, Extreme Range: 172 degrees
Number of Counties: 16 (plus 1 independent city)
POPULATION
Total: 911,000 (1984)
Rank: 43
Density: 8.3 persons per sq. mi.
Principal Cities: Las Vegas, 164,674; Reno, 100,756; North Las Vegas, 42,739; Sparks, 40,780; Carson City, 32,022; Henderson, 24,363; Boulder City, 9,590
EDUCATION
Schools: 292 elementary and secondary
Higher: 8
VITAL STATISTICS
Births (1980/83): 46,000
Deaths (1980/83): 20,000
Hospitals: 25
Drinking Age: 21
INTERESTING PEOPLE
Dat-So-La-Lee, Samuel Clemens (Mark Twain), James Warren Nye, William Morris Stewart, John A. Thompson, George Hearst, John Mackay, Winnemucca (chief), Paul Lexalt, Pat McCarran, Orion Clemens, James Fair
WHEN DID IT HAPPEN?
1826: Ogden explores
1829: Dat-So-La-Lee born
1843: Fremont-Carson explorations
1848: Nevada becomes part of U.S.
1849: Genoa (Mormon Station) first permanent settlement
1859: Boom begins on Comstock
1864: Statehood
1869: Continental railroad completed
1871: Capitol finished
1874: University of Nevada established
1900: Tonopah boom begins
1931: Gambling legalized
1936: Hoover Dam completed
1951: Atomic proving ground established
1959: Boulder City turned over to state control
1978: "Sagebrush Rebellion"
1980: Nevada leads nation in percentage of population growth

NEW MEXICO

FASCINATING NEW MEXICO

A group of Navajo men were trapped by Ute warriors. Their medicine men prayed for deliverance, and suddenly the ground under them took the form of a ship and sailed away, floating all day and all night until it came to land in a place the Navajo could call their own. According to this Navajo legend, that stony ship can still be seen on their reservation, and they call it Ship Rock.

New Mexico has many such colorful legends, but its actual past and present are alive with even more colorful sights, events and personalities.

The seven cities of gold were a mirage, but the fascinating ancient Pueblo civilizations were not, and their remains are among the most interesting relics of the past.

New Mexico can boast of the oldest skyscrapers, the oldest cooperative apartments and the oldest state capital. Many people in the state can recall one of the most historic events of all time, which happened in the New Mexico desert.

Interesting but less climactic were the symbolic canes, the explorers who arrived in silks and satins, and the railroad that took the name of a capital city and then passed it by.

Still to be seen are the miraculous circular stairway, the desert of glass and the tiny town with the most art per capita.

Natural historians marvel at the living cloud that comes and goes each day and the state bird that tags along, and miners have come to love the "mineral popcorn."

Out in the former wilderness where ancient peoples may have passed, today's visitors may hear the finest grand opera under the sky, illustrating one of the most interesting of all the fascinating contrasts of this fascinating land.

THE FACE OF NEW MEXICO

A tourist climbing up a breathtaking trail in the Sangre de Cristo Mountains would catch glimpses of wonderful scenery, with much of the fifth largest state spread out in view.

Eastward are the limitless plains and mesas stretching to Oklahoma and Texas. To the north loom other ranges of the Rocky Mountains, to the south the shining deserts, to the west perhaps the sparkling Rio Grande might come into view. Farther to the west are more great plains and mountain ranges.

New Mexico has six neighboring states, but only four are in the United States. The Mexican neighbors are the states of Chihuahua and Sonora. The entire western border is shared with Arizona. Colorado is on the north. The northern end of the eastern border touches Oklahoma, followed by a long border with Texas on the east. The Texas border takes a right angle and swings west to the Rio Grande River, where the river separates the two states for a short distance. This is the only natural boundary of New Mexico.

New Mexico and Utah do not have a common border, but they come together at a point at the Four Corners, the only place where four states meet together in one point.

At an elevation of 6,947 feet, Santa Fe is the highest capital city in the United States.

The Continental Divide cuts entirely through western New Mexico, wriggling like a snake as it runs from north to south. The Gila and San Juan rivers start west of this divide and flow into the Colorado River, which finally reaches the Pacific.

The Cimarron and Canadian rivers join the Mississippi system. The lengthy Rio Grande River begins in Colorado, divides New Mexico into nearly equal halves and enters Texas at the border. The Pecos is the largest river originating in New Mexico.

Only one state has a smaller area of natural lakes, only about 155 square miles for New Mexico. But rivers have been dammed to form numerous reservoirs. The largest of them is Elephant Butte Reservoir on the Rio Grande.

Rainfall is not plentiful in New Mexico, a dry state. Because it is a southern state, New Mexico might be expected to have a warm climate. However, the climate of an area is affected by its height above sea level. Because its lowest point is more than 2,800 feet, the state generally has a moderate to cool climate. It is interesting to note that in New Mexico the temperature falls 5 degrees for every 1,000-foot increase in elevation.

Although now high and dry, New Mexico was buried beneath ancient seas not once but several times. This was due to the great pressures deep in the earth, first pushing the land up, then letting it down below sea level. This process began

about 600,000,000 years ago. Evidence of this is shown in the fossils of sea creatures now found on the tops of mountains.

Finally, the pressures became so great that the Rocky Mountains were pushed up. The Rockies are among the youngest of all great ranges. However, the Sandia Mountains are very old, perhaps dating back 300,000,000 years.

Volcanoes have been active in New Mexico until as recently as 1,000 years ago. They have left their deposits on the plains adjoining Grants, Carrizoso, Capulin and other regions.

New Mexico is rich in fossils—dinosaurs, turtles, fish and amphibians.

EARLY DWELLERS

Remains of people have been found in New Mexico dating back 25,000 years. Because the remains were found in the Sandia Mountains, the very early dwellers were known as Sandia people. Later cavemen were called Folsom people. They hunted and killed great prehistoric animals, mastodons, mammals and giant sloths.

At a still later date, people known as the Basketmakers roamed about the state gathering seeds and nuts. As time went on, they learned how to cultivate crops and settled down in primitive houses, with the lower parts dug into the ground.

A visitor to present Chaco Canyon in 1150 A.D. would have passed along a well-kept road. He would pass laborers carrying heavy timbers from a forest 30 miles away, would note farmers tending their cornfields and boys and girls herding flocks of turkeys. The visitor might have been amazed to approach a good-sized city, with stone walls rising as high as five stories.

Opposite, Santa Fe

"Pueblo of Acoma," painting by Charles H. Harmon

That city is now known as Pueblo Bonito. The huge apartment buildings may have had as many as 800 apartments giving shelter to perhaps 1,500 people. The stone masonry work is said to be the finest prehistoric work north of Mexico. The Pueblo people who built these structures created a style of living still popular today.

Pueblo culture is divided into five periods. In the first two, skills as farmers, herders and builders of stone and adobe structures were developed. They reached their peak during period three, about 900 to 1200 A.D. Decline began in period four, probably because of a long drought, combined with attacks from outside tribes. Eventually, most of the splendid cities were abandoned.

During period five, the Pueblo peoples became known to modern history, and some of the ancient pueblos are inhabited by their descendants even today.

Astonishing skills in art and crafts were developed by the Pueblo peoples. Almost every girl learned to fashion beautiful pottery, which was painted or carved by the men and boys with traditional designs.

Much of the pottery that remains from ancient times is as beautiful as any that can be made today. In fact, the descendants of the Pueblo people are still noted for their wonderful pottery in both old and modern styles.

Every village had a large, round, sunken, walled area where religious rites as well as "town hall" style meetings and other gatherings were held. This was called a kiva.

The sand paintings of today probably were developed from the paintings made by the Pueblos, who used cornmeal dyed in various colors.

Pueblo peoples were peaceful and enjoyed their permanent homes. Their neighbors were quite different—warlike Indian nomads. These Athabascan tribes had moved south and were divided into two main groups—Navajo and Apache.

As time went by, the Navajo learned a great deal from the Pueblos and became somewhat more settled, building small houses, called hogans, of rock, logs and adobe. On the hunt they used huts made of brush and sticks; sometimes they

THAT'S CURIOUS:
The Indians said that the buffalo provided the weapon for their own death because the sinews were used as strings on their bows.

traded buffalo meat for the corn of the Pueblos, since buffalo were almost unknown in Pueblo territory.

At a later date the Apache, too, became more settled in much the same manner as the Navajo.

The Comanche and the Ute followed the great buffalo herds, hunting on foot until horses were introduced by the Europeans.

Buffalo meat was dried in the sun, mixed with herbs, fat and berries. Called pemmican, this food could be kept for a long time.

STIRRINGS

In 1536 shipwrecked Nunez Cabeza de Vaca and three companions struggled across present New Mexico with much hardship. Back in Mexico, they told stories of cities of gold. Sent to find these treasures in 1539, Marcos de Niza also brought back imaginary stories of wealth.

The great expedition of Francisco Vasquez de Coronado was sent next, in 1540, to discover and loot the golden Seven Cities of Cibola reported earlier.

Although he made some of the great discoveries of all time, Coronado returned to Mexico in disgrace, without any wealth of gold. The name Nuevo Mejico (New Mexico) was given to the area by Francisco de Ibarra in 1554.

At staggering expense from his own funds, youthful Don Juan de Onate brought together an enormous expedition including 7,000 head of livestock, 400 soldiers and settlers, along with 17 aristocratic Spanish ladies in silks and satins.

Onate established the first European settlement. The Indians revolted and killed Onate's nephew. He besieged the fortress of Acoma Pueblo and conquered the supposedly impregnable town. When his wealth gave out, Onate returned to Mexico.

In 1609 Don Pedro de Peralta founded the oldest capital city in the United States, which he called La Villa Real de la Santa Fe de San Francisco, now simply called Santa Fe.

Franciscan fathers established 43 churches and converted 34,000 Indians, and within 50 years Santa Fe was flourishing. Because of Spanish cruelties, there were Indian uprisings, harshly put down. In 1680 the Indians united under To-pa-tu, governor of the Picuris Pueblo. Four hundred Spaniards were killed, and Santa Fe was besieged.

The Indians drove the Spanish out and took over Santa Fe as their own capital. This was perhaps the greatest Indian victory in American history.

But the triumph did not last; the Spanish returned under Don Diego de Vargas and recaptured Santa Fe in 1692. In 1706 a village was founded in honor of the Duke of Alburquerque. With a slight change of spelling, this became Albuquerque, largest city in present New Mexico.

The plains Indians continued to harrass the Spanish settlements and the Pueblos. Then the United States bought all of Louisiana Territory and the Spanish worried that the young country might take over Spanish claims in the southwest, and restrictions were placed on U.S. visits.

In 1821, when Mexico became independent of Spain and controlled New Mexico, the restrictions were lifted. As the first train of wagons rumbled in from the U.S., the people of Santa Fe went wild: "Los Americanos! Los Carros! La

"The Old Santa Fe Trail," by Herbert Dunston

entrade de la caravana!" The year was 1822, and with terrible hardship all the way, the intrepid American traders had blazed the Santa Fe Trail from Missouri. The profit was worth all the hardship. Plump Spanish matrons (Senoras) willingly paid $3.00 a yard for calico that cost only a few cents. Items that were plentiful in St. Louis could be sold for much higher prices. The Santa Fe Trail became one of the great trade routes of the world.

The people of New Mexico revolted in 1837, but they were put down. Then in 1846, during the war with Mexico, U.S. forces under Stephen Watts Kearny captured Santa Fe without a fight. After a small battle at Brazito on Christmas Day, New Mexico came under U.S. control.

In the Civil War the Confederates claimed New Mexico and captured Albuquerque in 1862, but Union forces soon recaptured the area. Federal forces were victorious in the Battle of Glorietta near Santa Fe. This prevented the fall of Fort Union and saved the southwest for the Union.

During the war a group of Pueblo governors went to Washington to meet with President Lincoln. He assured them that the U.S. would honor the age-old boundaries of their territories.

Indian attacks were numerous and deadly during and after the Civil War. Names of the Indian leaders became well known to people throughout the country. Geronimo, Victorio, Cochise and others are still remembered for their fierce and often able leadership.

Indian attacks were not the only fears. Bandits and outlaws roamed the countryside, often more terrible and certainly more evil than the Indians, who felt they were protecting their own lands.

Billy the Kid, Saw Dust Charlie, Pock-marked Kid and J.J. Harlin were among the most notorious of those outlaws.

MIDDLE PERIOD

Often, groups of citizens known as vigilantes took the law into their own

THAT'S CURIOUS:
To show their authority, President Lincoln gave each of the Pueblo governors a silver-headed cane. These canes have been passed down from governor to governor and are highly prized as the symbols of the relationship of the Pueblos to the national government.

hands. They held hangings of outlaws which they called "necktie parties." With the capture of many outlaws and the surrender of Geronimo in 1886, the area began to feel more secure.

Mining, manufacturing, farming, communications and banking were important developments during the early decades of the 1900's.

Arizona rejected a 1906 plan to create a new state to include both New Mexico and Arizona, but six years later, on January 6, 1912, New Mexico became a state and claimed the 47th star in the U.S. flag. William C. McDonald was its first governor.

In 1916 New Mexico had its own little war. Mexican revolutionary leader Francisco "Pancho" Villa charged into the border town of Columbus with 1,000 followers. The burning of houses and killing of several residents prompted Washington to send General John J. Pershing to Columbus. The general led an expedition into Mexico to find Villa.

However, this little war was soon lost in the great battles of World War I. Beginning in 1917, New Mexico sent more than 15,000 men and women into service during the conflict in Europe.

New Mexico's state flag was selected by means of a contest in 1925. Dr. Harry Mera won the design contest, and his wife stitched up the first flag.

During World War II one of the most important events in world history took place in New Mexico. On July 16, 1945, there was a great explosion, and the world has never been the same since, nor will it ever be the same again. New Mexico's part of the story began in 1942 when the U.S. government took over the Los Alamos School for Boys to begin the most secret type of experimental work.

When that work had advanced sufficiently, the scientists were ready for a test. The small group watched breathlessly. Suddenly, the brightest manmade light ever seen was followed by an awesome cloud which quickly shot up in the shape of a mountain-sized mushroom.

The scientists at Los Alamos had succeeded in exploding the world's first atomic bomb. Later, it was found that the heat had been so awful that the sands under the bomb had turned to glass.

UP-TO-DATE

The awful war continued to call on men and women from New Mexico. A total of 73,000 served during the conflict, and 2,032 gave their lives.

Only three states are "younger" than New Mexico. Today its cities are modern in every way, but their traditions are age-old.

New Mexico has the broadest mixture of three of the most important cultures in America—Indian, Spanish and other Europeans. To them have been added more recent groups from all over the world.

From 1940 through 1982, the population has grown almost 300 percent.

Illustrating the appeal of the state as a whole in 1985, "Places-Rated Almanac" rated Albuquerque as one of the 25 best major metropolitan areas in the United States in which to live. Also in 1985, the Civil War Battle of Glorietta was reenacted near Sante Fe.

PERSONALITIES

For almost 40 years, a remarkable man, Padre Antonio Jose Martinez, struggled to make his beloved highland

PEOPLES

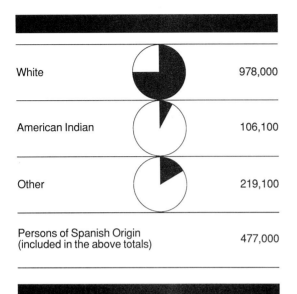

White	978,000
American Indian	106,100
Other	219,100
Persons of Spanish Origin (included in the above totals)	477,000

region a better place. He set up the first coeducational school in the southwest, established a newspaper and served in the territorial legislature. When the U.S. branch of the Catholic church took over, Monsignor Jean Baptiste Lamy took over. He disagreed with Father Martinez, who was defrocked and excommunicated. Bishop Lamy went on to rebuild many abandoned churches and to build 85 new ones, also improving the regional educational system. His life is celebrated in a well-known novel by Willa Cather. His death came in 1888, and this death forms the title of her novel.

The "bad" guys and the "good" guys played a large part in the history of New Mexico.

William H. Bonney became known as Billy the Kid. He is said to have killed first at the age of 12, and he seemed to enjoy killing. Jailed at one time, Billy starved himself for days, then wiggled through the bars of the jail and escaped. He was killed by the sheriff's forces at the old Maxwell House near Fort Sumner.

A noted lawman was Elfego Baca. As a deputy sheriff, he was holed up in a house by outlaws, but held them off, even as they aimed 3,000 shots at him, until he was rescued after 30 hours. This episode was made into a movie called "The Nine Lives of Elfego Baca."

The truest hero of the frontier was Christopher "Kit" Carson. He bluffed the Civil War Confederate supporters at Taos and went on to lead New Mexico volunteers in many Indian battles during the Civil War. Carson had come to New Mexico in 1826, was a cook, hunter and guide. He became famous as the unequalled guide and counselor for the noted explorer John C. Fremont. Famed for his courage, in one of his many feats Carson once made a hazardous trip through enemy lines during the War with Mexico. For his Civil War service, he was made a brigadier general in command of Fort Garland, Colorado. However, he always thought of Taos as home, and he was buried there in the cemetery named for him. He always stood out clearly for his modesty, integrity and ability.

Two famed writers spent relatively little time in New Mexico but they grew to love and appreciate the country. General Lew Wallace wrote "Ben Hur" during a period of government service in New Mexico. Famed writer D.H. Law-

THAT'S CURIOUS:
Outlaw Black Jack Ketchum was sentenced to be hanged. Just before the fatal event, he said to the hangman, "Hurry it up; I'm due in hell for dinner."

rence headquartered at Taos for two years and is buried there.

Oliver La Farge won the Pulitzer Prize for his "Laughing Boy, a Navajo Romance."

The crystal air and crisp dry climate of New Mexico have inspired artists from primitive times to the present—from the wonderful prehistoric cave paintings to the walls of art lining the dozens of galleries in Taos and Santa Fe today.

The most famous of the artists was Georgia O'Keeffe, who came to New Mexico after she had already gained fame. She loved her New Mexico ranch. When she died in Santa Fe in 1986 at the age of 98, she was recognized as one of the greatest artists of her time. She had become a living legend.

The best-known modern Pueblo potter was Maria Martinez, who carried the traditions of the Pueblo pottery to new heights. When she died in 1980, she too had become an artistic legend.

Indian sculptor Allan Houser creates large figures of Indian life and lore. Paul Flying Eagle Goodbear is another of the many talented and trained Indian artists; he specializes in paintings of ceremonial dances.

Ceramic worker Estella Loretto of Jemez Pueblo has managed to find new forms of artistic expression in her pottery. She says she creates "my interpretation of tradition and symbolic rituals in honor of the natural order of life."

Elizabeth Garrett, daughter of Sheriff Pat Garrett, wrote a song she called "O, Fair New Mexico." In an unusual session the state legislature heard her sing the song and chose it as New Mexico's official song.

One of the best-known men of his day was journalist-columnist Ernie Pyle of Albuquerque. Pyle was perhaps the best-known reporter of World War II. He lost his life in battle while reporting the conflict in the Pacific.

Jess Willard, another Santa Fe celebrity, became world heavyweight boxing champion in 1915.

A WEALTH OF NATURE

Some of the natural resources of New Mexico, such as timber, turquoise and salt, have been used for thousands of years. The value of others, such as uranium, has been discovered only in recent times.

Few states have as many kinds of minerals, at least 275 varieties. Only one county lacks signs of gas and oil deposits. There are rich sources of uranium, perlite, potassium salts, copper and molybdenum. The coal reserves might supply the nation's needs for a thousand years.

Iron ores, lead, zinc and some silver and gold are still to be found. Potash and fluorspar are said to be almost limitless.

Carbon dioxide is a valuable gas. Most people have never heard of lepidolite, but this New Mexico mineral has a part in the process of making shatter-proof glass.

Rock hounds find New Mexico a paradise of gems.

The "cow with frizzled hair," as the Spanish described the buffalo, is long gone, but herds of antelope, elk and mule deer roam the nearly 40,000,000 acres of public lands in the state. The state is a fisherman's delight.

The bats of Carlsbad Caverns are a natural wonder, said to number more than 5,000,000. Another interesting creature is the gila monster, a poisonous lizard.

The state bird of New Mexico is known as the roadrunner because it streaks along, tail raised, head lowered, often keeping pace with a car. Their foot-wide nests are firmly planted in the crooks of large cacti.

Because New Mexico stretches over six of the seven life zones of North America, more than 6,000 types of grasses, trees, plants and flowers grow in the state. The schoolchildren of New Mexico selected the yucca eleta as the state flower in 1927.

Indians used the yucca to make a kind of soap, and today its fibers are used in making bags and twine.

USING THE WEALTH

In agriculture, livestock is still the principal source of income. The first settlers under Onate pioneered the nation's livestock industry. Today vast herds of cattle and sheep roam the nearly 50 million acres of rangeland. Among other claims to agricultural fame, New Mexico boasts the "largest goose farm in the world."

Cotton is the most important crop, along with hay, sorghum and commercial vegetables. Also grown in quantity are wheat, peanuts, broomcorn, barley and pecans. One of the largest pecan orchards anywhere is found near Mesilla.

Brilliant red fields of chili peppers, as well as rows of peppers drying on racks, attract visitors. Bright strings of chilis can be seen hanging on many a door frame. Chili pepper is an official state vegetable.

In mining, New Mexico ranks first among the states in potash. That industry began in 1931 and is still expanding. This fertilizing material has given Carlsbad unofficial rank as potash capital of America.

Much of the growth of southeast New Mexico has been due to the potash boom.

Perlite is sometimes called "mineral popcorn." It makes lighter concrete and plaster. Eighty percent of all U.S. perlite comes from New Mexico, mostly around the Seven Hills of Taos area.

New Mexico is second in the nation in uranium production. It is interesting to note that Navajo Indians have sold many millions of dollars worth of uranium since they began mining in 1952.

New Mexico's oil production began in 1909. Today much of the oil is in Indian territory, producing substantial income. Some of the state's oil is considered to be the finest grade.

New Mexico always ranks high among the states in natural gas. Helium is produced at the Navajo plant, and the state produces most of the nation's carbon dioxide.

Copper mining began in 1800. When the higher grade gave out, new methods allowed the use of the vast supplies of lower grade ore in the state.

Coal, pumice, turquoise and salt are important.

More than 6 million acres of forest are classified as commercial timber, and lumber and wood products are prominent in manufacturing. Albuquerque has become a leader in space age industries.

In New Mexico it is possible to travel on the oldest highway in the United States, pioneered by the Spanish as early as 1581 and named El Camino Real, or the King's Highway. Later, the most important trade route was the Santa Fe Trail. The Santa Fe railroad had the city's name in its title, but it bypassed the capital when it crossed the state in the 1880's.

GETTING AROUND

New Mexico has many sites set aside by the national government, ranging from abandoned forts to the remains of ancient civilizations.

Cowboy Jim White was amazed that day in 1901. The ground appeared to be smoking. Looking closely, he saw that the cloud was formed by millions of bats emerging from a hole in the ground. That hole was a great cave, now Carlsbad Caverns National Park, one of the world's largest caves. The bats still leave every evening and return every morning to the delight of tourists.

The only fully restored great kiva on the continent is found at Aztec Ruins National Monument. Another twelfth-century ruin is Bandelier National Monument, resting in one of the largest of all volcanic craters. At one time, Bandelier could boast the largest apartment building in the country. Gila Cliff Dwellings National Monument is almost lost in vast Gila National Forest.

More recent ruins are those of Fort Union National Monument.

Nature has not been overlooked in other national monuments. The gleaming

THE ECONOMY

in millions of $

Mining	5,520
Manufacturing	3,069
Agriculture	2,927
Service	2,408
Tourism	1,470

Principal Products:

primary metals, petroleum, food

Agriculture:

cattle, wheat, corn, dairy products

undulations of White Sands National Monument form a unique desert of silica, raw material of glass. From the top of Capulin Mountain's almost perfect cone, five states can be seen if conditions are right.

There also are a number of national wildlife refuges and recreation sites, preserving interesting and valuable areas.

One of the nation's most fascinating communities, Taos is really three distinct communities—the Pueblo, Ranchos de Taos (an Indian farming community) and Taos, the county seat. The modern version of the old Spanish village still centers on the square, where famed artists and writers, dress designers and artisans mingle with the tourists. There may be more than 100 well-known artists living in the area.

Today, some of the galleries of Taos are among the finest to be found outside

"Evening at Pueblo Taos," by Ernest A. Blumenschein

a great metropolitan area, with over 80 galleries in the tiny town.

The strange dugout-style home of Kit Carson outside the town has been kept as a memorial.

One of the most interesting places in the country is Taos Pueblo. Outside, the buildings have been kept much as they were for hundreds of years. This is said to be the oldest cooperative apartment complex in the United States. Visitors, who enter for a small fee, are amazed by the quality and beauty of the buildings and the scenes of life, some dating back to prehistoric times.

In addition to Taos, New Mexico is proud of its eighteen other occupied pueblos, each with some particular attraction of its own. Most pueblos have feast days, with dances and processions.

In everyday life some old customs are still carried on.

Many of the old communities are no longer occupied. More than 25,000 ruined sites have been found in New Mexico.

Albuquerque was dedicated in 1706 with the old Spanish custom of tossing stones to the four corners of the compass.

The town grew around the central plaza, then spread out into other areas, so that it is divided into New Town and Old Town.

Today much of the flavor of Old Town has been restored. The four-foot-thick walls of San Felipe de Neri Church still protect the worshippers. Colorful crowds still mingle in the plaza—Indians in blankets, cowboys, atomic scientists and tourists. Wonderful treasures of Indian jewelry, rugs and pottery are for sale in the many shops. Working artists and craftsmen, art exhibits and sales, summer theater and the sound of guitar music all lend their charm.

The federal government has more than 100 agencies in the Albuquerque area, including Sandia Base, the Air Force Special Weapons Center and Defense Atomic Support Agency.

The University of New Mexico at Albuquerque is a center of learning and a focus of community theater and music.

Other attractions of New Mexico include the Navajo reservation, with Shiprock looming above, the famous Inscription Rock where famed explorers carved their names and the town of Bell perched atop a 20-mile-long mesa. Near Cloudcroft is Sunspot on Sacramento Peak, the world's largest center for studying the sun. Cloudcroft's golf course is said to be the highest in the world.

The resort of Ruidoso boasts its great skiing and the richest horse race in America.

Hot-air ballooning, panning for gold, horseback trails, hunting, snowmobiling, spelunking, off-road motoring and the traditional dances and festivals all add to the state's attractions. The deer dance at Tesuque and the animal dance of the Peccas Indians are among the most interesting Indian festivals.

Five different flags have flown over Santa Fe, one of the most interesting cities of the country. Fascinating reminders of the earlier periods—Spanish, Indian Federation, Mexican, Confederate eras—still abound.

The capital city is a world center of art, with dozens of galleries and many fine artists in the area working in every style and medium.

People, even in remote lands, who know about music have heard about Santa Fe. It all began in 1955 when the Santa Fe Opera Association determined to present quality opera in the city. Today, opera lovers from all over the world gather in an open pavillion to hear "Opera under the stars," presented with the great singing stars and productions to equal any other.

The present capitol was built in 1900, with additions and remodeling in 1922 and 1951-1953. It is generally considered to be the only U.S. state capitol built in the style of its territorial days.

Life still centers on the plaza, where the adobe structure, the Palace of the Governors, is the oldest public building in use in the U.S. It is now a museum with treasures of the past.

The oldest church in the nation is the Church of San Miguel.

Since 1712, Santa Fe has celebrated the Fiesta de Santa Fe, one of the nation's great festivals. Reenactment of the city's founding, ancient tribal dancing, parades, Indian market and other attractions provide a unique introduction to this fascinating state with its combination of ancient and modern cultures.

THAT'S CURIOUS:
When the Lady of Light Chapel was built at Santa Fe, there seemed to be no room for a staircase. Suddenly, as if in answer to prayer, a stranger appeared and built a circular stairway in about six months. He had solved a problem thought to be without solution. He disappeared as suddenly as he had arrived, but the staircase is still much admired.

The capitol

COMPAC-FACS

NEW MEXICO
Land of Enchantment

HISTORY
Statehood: January 6, 1912
Admitted as: 47th state
Capital: Sante Fe, settled 1609
OFFICIAL SYMBOLS
Motto: Crescit Eunde (It grows as it goes)
Animal: Black Bear
Bird: Roadrunner
Fish: Cutthroat trout
Flower: Yucca elata
Tree: Pinon pine
Vegetables: Chile and frijol
Gem: Turquoise
Colors: Red and yellow of old Spain
Song: "O, Fair New Mexico," by Elizabeth Garrett
Spanish Language Song: "Asi Es Nuevo Mejico"
GEO-FACS
Area: 121,593 sq. ft.
Rank in Area: 5th
Length (n/s): 390 mi.

Width (e/w): 350 mi.
Geographic Center: 12 mi SSW of Willard
Highest Point: 13,161 ft. (Wheeler Peak)
Lowest Point: 2,817 ft. (Red Bluff Reservoir)
Mean Elevation: 5,700 ft.
Temperature, Extreme Range: 166 degrees
Number of Counties: 33
POPULATION
Total: 1,424,000 (1984)
Rank: 37th
Density: 11.7 persons per sq. mi.
Principal Cities: Albuquerque, 331,767; Santa Fe, 48,953; Las Cruces, 45,086; Roswell, 39,676; Farmington, 31,222; Clovis, 31,194; Hobbs, 29,153
EDUCATION
Schools: 635 elementary and secondary
Higher: 20
VITAL STATISTICS
Births (1980/83): 88,000
Deaths (1980/83): 29,000
Hospitals: 57
Drinking Age: 21
INTERESTING PEOPLE
Antonio Jose Martinez, Jean Baptiste Lamy, Bill Mauldin, Georgia O'Keeffe, Elfego Baca, Christopher (Kit) Carson, Oliver La Farge, D.H. Lawrence, Allan Houser, Estella Loretto, Jess Willard, Ernie Pyle, Peter Hurd
WHEN DID IT HAPPEN?
1536: De Vaca party crosses
1539: De Niza claims for Spain
1540: Coronado explores
1580: Rodriguez explores
1598: Onate begins colonization
1609: Santa Fe founded
1706: Alburquerque (Albuquerque) founded
1807: Pike explores
1821: Mexico takes over
1833: Sante Fe Trail inaugurated
1846: U.S. takes over
1850: New Mexico Territory formed
1862: Civil War comes to New Mexico
1881: Railroad crosses state
1901: Carlsbad Caverns found
1912: Statehood
1917: World War I calls 17,157
1941: Heroic New Mexico National Guard on Bataan
1945: History's first atomic explosion
1982: Population growth 300% in 40 years
1985: Albuquerque rated among 25 best cities

UTAH

FASCINATING UTAH

It was the land nobody wanted. It was the land the founder selected because he was sure no one would drive his people out in order to seize the land for themselves.

Then from this "worthless" land came miracles of settlement. Crops flourished; new communities sprang up on barren soil; thousands of travelers were fed and helped on their way—all through the strength and religious determination of the settlers.

Throughout that "worthless" land, discoveries were made of some of the most awe-inspiring scenery on the planet, a land full of features found nowhere else.

That no longer useless land is Utah, the land where many regions still have not been explored, where new wonders may still be found.

It also is a land of smaller mysteries and fascinations, the home of the original "honest Injuns," the place of the pickled buffalo, the stolen symbol of the Navajo, a desert full of pelicans and seagulls.

Its history tells why the people erected a monument to those seagulls and recounts the story of the "business" conventions held in the wilderness, of the governor who missed the point.

For reasons both great and small, Utah is truly a fascinating land.

THE FACE OF UTAH

"Wonderful, outrageous, mysterious and strange" exclaimed a recent visitor to Utah. The geography of the state fully bears out such extravagant appraisal.

Utah has more varied and unique features of geography than any other state. Yet, even today, many of these wonders probably have not been discovered or made known. The region of Kaiparowits Plateau is thought to be the largest area in the United States that has not been thoroughly explored.

Some of the natural features have worldwide fame, but there are so many others of almost equal interest that whole volumes are needed just to describe them.

Every force of nature has worked on the surface of Utah to create its multitude of wonders. On four separate occasions forces beneath the surface have pushed up the land. Each time, parts of the surface were worn away by wind and water taking weird and dramatic shapes.

Most recently (from 50,000 years ago to about 10,000 years ago), the melting glaciers rearranged the landscape, covering huge areas with lakes. The largest of these prehistoric lakes was named Lake Bonneville. At its greatest extent it lay over much of northern Utah into present Nevada. As the waters dried up, the lake diminished in size, leaving terrace ledges to mark its former boundaries. Utah's principal cities are now perched on those terraces. Great Salt Lake and Little Salt Lake are all that remain of that vast prehistoric lake. The Bonneville Salt Flats stretch along its former bed.

In other places wind and water have carved deep canyons into the surface, exposing rocks that date back before life on earth.

Almost everywhere, nature's sculpture has been at work. Sometimes a stream would cut through a mountain, as in Big Cottonwood Canyon near Salt Lake City. Other canyons were formed by

THAT'S CURIOUS:

At the Zion Narrows, the Virgin River Canyon is so narrow and so deep that even in bright daylight, those looking up at the sky from the bottom can see the stars.

eroding, deepening and widening of the canyon by the stream or river. Virgin River Canyon near St. George is an "eroded" type of Canyon. The canyons are among the most spectacular of nature's formation in the state, reaching a crescendo in the spectacular reaches of Zion National Park. Also spectacular, almost to the point of being unreal, are the vast arches of the natural bridges (many of which are still uncharted), the peaks and spires of Monument Valley and the "most colorful twenty miles in the world," as someone described Bryce Canyon National Park.

Bryce is not really a canyon but rather an escarpment.

No other area of Utah's size can boast so many natural bridges. Rainbow Bridge is the largest and best known. Its name comes from the Indian legend that a rainbow was turned into stone to provide a group of gods with a bridge over a flood.

Even the rivers of Utah are unusual. Bear River is the longest river in the Western Hemisphere which does not eventually reach the ocean. Flowing for 500 miles, it covers only about 90 airline miles before flowing into Great Salt Lake. The Bear is only one of many such rivers because much of Utah lies in what is known as the Great Basin. None of the waters emptying into this basin get to the sea.

Two of the country's great rivers cut through Utah. The Colorado River surges across the southwest corner; one of its major tributaries is the Green, which enters Utah from the north, crosses into Colorado, then crosses back into Utah, where it runs across most of the state to empty into the Colorado.

In Utah the major southern tributary of the Colorado is the San Juan. Near Mexican Hat, the San Juan takes a series of U-turns which are known as goosenecks, or "entrenched meanders." This is considered the best example in the world of such meanders.

The Sevier River is the longest of the kind that simply end without emptying into any other river or body of water. It disappears into the dry bed of Sevier Lake.

Great Salt Lake is an extraordinary body of water. Because it has no outlet, the salty minerals brought into it from the mountain streams make the lake the second most salty in the world. In the 1980's the water level began to rise dramatically, overflowing much of the region around and causing great damage.

Quite different are the very fresh waters of Utah Lake, a welcome relief from the dry land all around. Bear Lake has its very own monster, a legendary sea serpent.

Glen Canyon Dam is in Arizona, but most of the water of Lake Powell is backed far up into Utah, providing another wonderful reservoir of fresh water for a thirsty land. Far to the north, the Green River is dammed to form Flaming Gorge Reservoir, which extends into Wyoming.

The waters of lakes and rivers originate in the mountains as snow and

Opposite, Salt Lake City

99

Bryce Canyon

rain. The state is dotted with ranges; the two most important are the Wasatch and the Uintas. In still another example of Utah's unique geography, the Uintas are the only U.S. range that runs east and west. Still another unique feature is the San Rafael Swell, said to be one of the country's major geological wonders.

Much of Utah is made up of little-explored desert or primitive areas. The Great Salt Lake Desert took its toll of many a weary traveler. Today's better-equipped traveler finds beauty in the Painted Desert and the Coral Pink Sand Dunes.

Altogether, Utah is "one of the most picturesque and scenic areas on earth."

EARLY DWELLERS

Even today, the blackened smudges of prehistoric campfires can be seen at the base of Rainbow Bridge. These dark markings provide one of the relatively few traces left behind by the earliest people in what is now Utah.

The prehistoric peoples are known by the general term of Anasazi, or ancient ones. The earliest traces are stone weapons and other primitive objects of perhaps 10,000 years ago. By 1,500 years ago the people had become more advanced, cultivating corn and beans, storing the grain in pits lined with adobe bricks. As the population grew, large communities of adobe were built by the Pueblo people of the southern area. When they built their communities in caves or clefts in the rocks, they were known as Cliff Dwellers.

The Pueblo peoples developed a high degree of civilization, with special skills in basket making, beautifully decorated fur robes, handsome jewelry and woven fur blankets, among others. Most of the Pueblo communities were abandoned for reasons that are not yet quite clear.

Southern Arizona has many relics of their fascinating civilization. An adobe village near Monticello, Zion cliff ruins and a rock fort in Nine Mile Canyon near Price show the extraordinary level of their culture. The latter is the most northerly cliff dwelling ruin.

Ancient artists left drawings and carvings on rock walls, such as the big murals of Barrier Canyon and the drawings on Newspaper Rock. One of them is a balloon-like figure enhanced by bright colors.

By the time Europeans had reached the area, the Ute, Paiute and Shoshone Indians were living in parts of present Utah. The Eutaw tribe has given the state its name, which probably means

100

"people who live on the high places."

For the Indians, making a living from the rough land was hard; they were less warlike than many of the western tribes. A good part of their time had to be spent in gathering food. Rabbits provided both food and fur for clothing and blankets. They were not as advanced as the Indians to the east. The Gosiute were among the most primitive Indians on the continent. As T.J. Farnum described them in 1845, "They wear no clothing of any description—eat roots, lizards and snails...in winter...they dig holes...and sleep and fast till the weather permits them to go abroad again for food...these poor creatures are hunted in the spring...when weak and helpless...fattened, carried to Santa Fe and sold as slaves."

The Navajo who arrived in the area about 1500 A.D. were different from the other tribes. They spoke a language similar to that of the Athapascan of western Canada. These warlike, proud people still live on their vast reservations, a small part of which lies to the south and west of Utah.

STIRRINGS

When early travelers from Mexico reached the Colorado River, they thought the dusty lands to the north were useless, so little attention was paid to the area for decades. American independence had just been declared when the first Europeans of record reached present Utah in 1776. They were the Catholic fathers Silvestre de Escalante and Francisco Dominguez, leading a party to find a route from Santa Fe to Carmel, California.

The mighty Colorado River was a terrible barrier; finally they cut steps in the riverside. This was thought to be at a place that became known as the Crossing of the Fathers, but the real place was about a mile away at the mouth of Padre Creek.

The route they blazed became the "Old Spanish Trail," going north and west and then almost due west, following present Highway 91 in some places. The principal trade on this route was in the Indian slaves kidnapped by Spanish travelers along the way. This slave trade was not made illegal until 1852.

British fur trappers entered present Utah about 1819, with American trappers not far behind. In 1824 Jim Bridger was the first European to reach the shores of Great Salt Lake, although Etienne Provost had spotted it first from a distance; Bridger tasted the water and thought he had reached the Pacific Ocean.

The terrible winter described by Bridger almost exterminated the buffalo in Utah.

Peter Skene Ogden was another early visitor, and the present city of Ogden took his name. Provost's name was given to the river town of Provo.

Jedediah Strong Smith established a fur trading business in 1826, and he explored much of the area thoroughly, becoming the first person to pass overland across plains, mountains and desert from Missouri to California. Later, this extraordinary man crossed the Great

THAT'S CURIOUS:
The Indians of Utah had a reputation for honesty. Bishop Whipple of Minnesota asked a chief if his belongings would be safe in his tent if he left them for some time. The chief replied, "Yes, there is not a white man within a hundred miles."

Basin in the other direction and became a true authority on the area.

Antoine Robidoux made a fort in the 1830's which became the first European settlement in Utah. One of the most interesting "conventions" on record was held annually for a number of years. This was the Rendezvous of the trappers, often held in Utah. This colorful gathering was assembled at present Ogden in 1825-26, when a large group of trappers pitched their skin tents and enjoyed races, story telling, singing and games along with trading. The rendezvous were held until 1840.

The first immigrant group passed overland in 1841, with Nancy Kelsey, the first white woman in present Utah.

From 1843 through 1845, famed explorer John C. Fremont studied and mapped the area in a scientific way.

In 1845, with Kit Carson as guide, the Fremont group were the first white people to cross the central Salt Desert. Fremont has been credited with opening the west to general settlement. The first permanent white settlement in Utah was begun by Miles Goodyear in 1844-45 and named Fort Beunaventura.

UNIQUE PEOPLE, UNIQUE SAGA

The epic of settlement that followed must be considered one of the unique episodes of world history.

"This is the place; drive on," Brigham Young exclaimed, on July 24, 1847, and drive on they did to found one of history's most unusual communities. The place, of course, was the valley of Great Salt Lake.

Young made his famous comment on a hill overlooking present Salt Lake City.

Terror and persecution had driven the Mormons from all of the earlier homes they had built so well in various states to the east. Young hoped to find a place that would not be envied by any neighbors. The Salt Lake City area looked like a place no one else would want.

The Mormon migration to the west had started in 1846; more than 4,000 had wintered on the bluffs of the Missouri in eastern Iowa. While there, 500 young Mormon men formed the Mormon Battalion and marched west to take part in the War with Mexico. They made one of the most famous of all forced marches. The war was over by the time they reached California, but they had done much to pioneer the routes westward. They joined their relatives at the valley of the Salt Lake at about the same time the first groups arrived there from the east.

Before the main group had gotten in, an advance group had arrived under Orson Pratt. After a worship service of thanks, they dedicated the land to God. The next day, they dammed a small stream they called City Creek, "...commenced planting our potatoes after which we turned the water upon them and gave the ground quite a soaking," as Pratt wrote in his journal. Within a space of only two days they had worshipped, irrigated and planted. By fall of 1847, one thousand Mormons had made the difficult trek to Salt Lake City.

Their early crops were successful, and

THAT'S CURIOUS:

One winter was so severe that Jim Bridger said many buffalo were frozen. "All I had to do was tumble 'em into Salt Lake an' I had pickled buffalo enough for myself and the whole Ute nation for years."

North State Street, Salt Lake City, in the early days, by Don Weggeland

by the spring of 1858 they had planted about 5,000 more acres. Suddenly, a horde of insects zoomed in on the tender crops. "Never did I experience such a terrible time as when the crickets swept down upon our fields of grain to destroy them...and yet we knew God would deliver us," one pioneer wrote.

As suddenly as the crickets had arrived, a great flock of seagulls swooped in and devoured the insects.

More Mormons arrived. A fort was built; Young decided on the site of the temple; he ordered a city to be laid out in perfect squares, with each block contain-ing ten acres and with streets uniformly 132 feet wide. By 1849 they had estab-lished a provisional "State of Deseret," and flour mills and sawmills operated by waterpower had been built; crops were good, and progress continued.

When vast numbers of gold seekers on the way to California crossed the desert in 1849-50, the Mormon settle-ment seemed like a mirage. Here the weary 49'ers could trade things the Mormons needed for supplies the travel-ers required to continue the journey.

The accomplishments of the Mor-mons in sending out groups to occupy

THAT'S CURIOUS:

Young did not choose the site of his future city because of its beauty. According to wife Clara Decker Young, Brigham Young had said earlier, "'If there is a place on this earth that nobody else wants, that's the place'...I cried, for it seemed to me the most desolate in all the world."

other desolate areas seem almost incredible. Farmington and Bountiful were settled in the same year as Salt Lake City. Within eight years they had established 14 communities in Utah, California and Nevada. Among them were Ogden and Provo, San Bernardino in California and Las Vegas in Nevada.

They accomplished all this because of a religious devotion to duty as they saw it in an "epic story of hardship, sacrifice, failure and triumph."

However, the civilization they had hoped to avoid was already creeping in. The Territory of Utah was created in 1850, with Brigham Young as territorial governor, in spite of the suspicions of him held by outsiders.

Almost from the beginning, the Mormons had sent missionaries to other countries. Now hundreds of their converts were arriving in America at the end of the railroads, looking for means of crossing the rest of the country to their promised land. Most of them could not afford wagons and draft animals, so Young sent handcarts and guides, and incredible numbers struggled across country, pulling carts with meager possessions, marooned at times in winter snows and often without food.

In Utah Indian troubles continued through the "Walker War," led by Chief Walker, but the major Indian troubles ended with Ute Black Hawk War in 1868. Much greater trouble was to come with the United States government. U.S. troops moved in to put down what the

government called a "Mormon Rebellion." The Mormons were almost ready to move out again when affairs were settled.

One of the major concerns of "outsiders" was the official Mormon acceptance of polygamy, of permitting more than one wife. The federal government outlawed this practice and dissolved the church corporation. Brigham Young died in 1877, but his successors continued to have difficulties. In 1884 12,000 Mormons lost citizenship because of polygamy. Then in 1890, the church ruled against polygamy, and all rights were returned.

Suspicions of the Mormons had long kept Utah from becoming a state, but this was finally achieved in 1896, with a constitution guaranteeing religious freedom, and outlawing polygamy.

UP-TO-DATE

Progress continued with the opening of the railroad trestle across part of Great Salt Lake in 1903. Progress of another kind was made with the discovery of Rainbow Bridge in 1909.

During World War I, 20,000 Utahans saw service, and the thrifty Mormons were in position to make substantial contributions of grain and other supplies to starving European nations.

World War II called 70,000 Utah men and women into service.

The decades that followed brought more growth in the economy and enor-

---

THAT'S CURIOUS:
The seagulls' part in saving the first crop was so appreciated that the bird holds a special place in Mormon thinking. In Temple Square at Salt Lake City a handsome memorial to the seagull now greets all visitors.

mous growth in the worldwide membership of the Mormon church centered at Salt Lake City. A skyscraper headquarters for this multinational organization and many other improvements, such as a multimillion dollar arts center, added to the city's growth.

Disaster came in 1983 when some of the heaviest rains and snowfalls on record brought the most widespread flooding in the region's history. The streets of Salt Lake City became torrents, and temporary bridges were built over them. The city recovered quickly, but the levels of Great Salt Lake continued to rise (ten feet in only two years), bringing even greater property damage.

In 1985 copper mining in Utah ceased after 82 successful years. However, tourism continued to increase as more and more people worldwide became familiar with the unique attractions of the state.

PERSONALITIES

"One of the major figures in western history, a man of enormous energy and vision," perhaps even "the most brilliant genius in the development of the American West," was one description of Brigham Young.

This unique personality was born in Vermont in 1801. He was one of the first twelve Mormon leaders, and became the principal Mormon leader in 1835 when Joseph Smith was assassinated.

Young's genius as a colonizer resulted in the founding of 350 Mormon colonies, probably a record for one man's planning. He gave constant attention to each, as well as conducting the innumerable businesses of the church and creating

PEOPLES

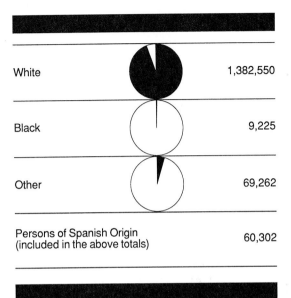

White	1,382,550
Black	9,225
Other	69,262
Persons of Spanish Origin (included in the above totals)	60,302

new ideas in many fields. To all this was added the care of his 27 wives.

Young developed substantial philosophies of government and education as well as religion. His 30-year stay in Utah provides a record of unparalleled achievement. Overall, one researcher concludes, "I know of no instance where he acted unreasonably, or unfairly, or impractically."

Appropriately, Utah was the birthplace of "Western" style fiction. Author Zane Grey learned all about the life of the west, its roping and riding, and roundups and villains while living in Utah. His book "Riders of the Purple Sage" set the pattern for most of the thousands of "Westerns" that followed.

Other prominent Utah authors in-

THAT'S CURIOUS:
When the Nazis adopted the swastika as their symbol of hatred, the loyal Navajo banned their ancient symbol of friendship which so closely resembled the swastika.

clude Phillis McGinley and Bernard De Voto.

Sculptor Mahonri Young, Brigham Young's grandson, created the lovely Seagull Monument and the mammoth "This Is the Place" monument, dedicated in 1947, at the Emigration Canyon site where Young originally made that cry.

A one-armed explorer-scientist, John Wesley Powell, made great contributions to both Utah and America in geology and exploration. He led the first party, nine men and four boats, down the Green River and into the Colorado River. After conquering the terrible rapids of the Grand Canyon, the party made the difficult climb up the canyon wall and the exhausting journey across 300 miles of wilderness to reach Salt Lake City in 1869. Lake Powell bears his name.

Powell's careful notes provide some of the best early descriptions of Utah, "...a strange, weird, grand region. The landscape, everywhere away from the river, is of rock; crags of rock—ten thousand strangely carved forms—rocks everywhere, and no vegetation, no soil, no sand...a whole land of naked rock, with giant forms carved on it; cathedral shaped buttes, towering hundreds or thousands of feet; cliffs that cannot be scaled, and canyon walls that shrink the river into insignificance, with vast, hollow domes, and tall pinnacles...all highly colored—buff, gray, red, brown, and chocolate, never lichened; never moss-covered, but bare, and often polished."

Several Utah inventors have contributed to human welfare. They include Philo T. Farnsworth, described as "the most important single person in the development of television," including the picture tube. He was only 21 in 1927 when he demonstrated his first television system.

John M. and Jonathan Browning of Ogden were noted developers of automatic weapons. More humanely, Dr. Harvey Fletcher of Provo became "the patron saint of the hard-of-hearing" when he invented various testing and hearing aids for the deaf.

John Henry Seely was recognized widely for his development in livestock breeding.

Among leaders of America's Indians, Chief Kanosh of the Pahvants was called by Levi Edgar Young "one of the noblest Indians that ever lived." Chief Washakie was another "great and good chief," who "helped many companies of emigrants on their way to Utah."

On the other hand, one of the greatest friends of the Indians was Jacob Hamblin, a leader in southern Utah settlement. His nine rules for dealing with the Indians might well be followed in human association of any kind.

Secretary of War under F.D. Roosevelt was former Utah governor, George E. Dern. Mrs. Ivy Baker Priest was Treasurer of the United States.

Ezra Taft Benson was Secretary of Agriculture under President Dwight D. Eisenhower. He was a long-time leader in the Mormon church and succeeded to the principal leadership in 1986.

A WEALTH OF NATURE

Levi Edgar Young called Utah "...the treasure house of the nation."

From that treasure, Utah salt could meet the needs of the entire world for 1,000 years, as well as the world's coal demands for 200 years. Helium and other natural gas, carbon dioxide and asphalt are a part of the mineral store. One of the treasures for future use is the enormous deposit of oil shale.

One of the best insulating materials is the rare Ozokerite, found elsewhere only in Austria.

Semiprecious stones include opal, garnet, topaz, jet and jasper.

Water is the most precious mineral and the one in shortest supply.

Scattered among the vast dry stretches, surprisingly, every one of Utah's counties has forest lands, with about three million acres of commercial quality. Ponderosa is the most used of the commercial timbers.

The Indians used the pinon pine nut as food, the sticky gum as waterproofing, as well as many other uses. Some of the bristlecone pines have lately come to be considered the oldest living things on earth.

The spring flowers of the state vary from the showy white columbine to the many desert cacti. The datura plant puts forth a creamy night blossom in Zion Canyon.

The bulb of the state flower, sego lily, provided meal for flour for the Indians or was eaten boiled. Mormon pioneers called the Joshua trees (really members of the lily family) by that name because they thought the plants looked like Joshua at prayer.

Large deer herds, Rocky Mountain sheep and pronghorn antelope are still to be found, along with the beaver and marten.

Seagulls and pelicans are surprising members of the desert community.

USING THE WEALTH

Mile after mile, the tracks were laid down with unbelievable speed. The track workers were promised handsome bonuses for swift advances across the wilderness. The Union Pacific was coming from the east and the Central Pacific from the west. Seven years of work had been hampered by Indian attack, bad weather and lack of supplies, but on May 10, 1869, the long wait was over. The U.S. finally was connected by rail from coast to coast. Promontory Point in Utah was the place where the union was complete. High officials arrived for the celebration. The last tie was laid bearing a silver plate with inscription; engines moved slowly together from west and east. The driving of the last spike, of pure gold, activated telegraph keys across the country. At last, the continent had been bridged by swift rail transport.

A year later, a branch road was constructed south to Salt Lake City by a private company headed by Brigham Young. This was the first railroad in the country to be built without any kind of government subsidy. The Mormons were as thorough about the construction of good transportation routes as they were about all other phases of the economy.

However, their beliefs did not permit using precious minerals such as gold and silver, so the non-Mormons (Gentiles)

THAT'S CURIOUS:
Governor Leland Stanford of California swung the sledgehammer with a mighty blow—and missed the gold spike, the last link in the continental chain. However, the telegraph operator quickly pressed the key, and the word went out over the wires. Except for the governor's confusion, the day was saved.

THE ECONOMY

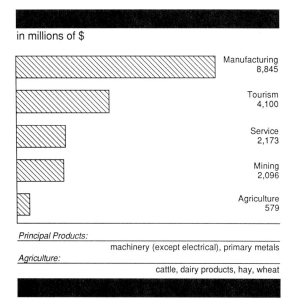

in millions of $

Manufacturing	8,845
Tourism	4,100
Service	2,173
Mining	2,096
Agriculture	579

Principal Products:

machinery (except electrical), primary metals

Agriculture:

cattle, dairy products, hay, wheat

took over the exploitation of the mineral wealth of the state.

Copper mining from the great open pits was the most spectacular, but as of this writing, that great industry has diminished. Gold, lead and silver are still produced along with oil and gas.

An unusual mineral is Gilsonite, named for its Utah discoverer. It now is used for fireproof insulation.

Iron-ore deposits were developed, with Provo as the most important steel center in the western states. Dolomite and limestone from the Payson area are used in steel processing.

Potash and uranium are also important. Coal is still second to petroleum in the state's mineral income, but Utah no longer ranks first in coal produced west of the Mississippi.

Almost as soon as the Mormons had arrived, home industry began to flourish. Soon meat products were being prepared

in hand-soldered tin cans. Processing of food products is still important, but the manufacture of machinery, processing of primary metals and production of transportation equipment are now the leading industries.

Almost from the beginning, the Mormons were able to transform land which for centuries was said to be useless. The first irrigation out of tiny City Creek has been expanded until more than 650 dams, reservoirs and mountain tunnels assure water for almost every inch of the 5 percent of Utah which is thought to be suitable for cultivation. When the Mormons found that irrigation was making the soil too alkaline to grow crops, they discovered a process called dry farming, producing crops in the dry region without irrigation.

An industry that has carried Utah's spectacular scenery all over the world is the production of motion pictures. The magnificent natural backdrops and the Old West setting of ghost towns and other picturesque locations have been used in many famous pictures.

This great attraction of the state for tourists has made tourism the second most important income source for the state.

GETTING AROUND

Southern and southeastern Utah possess an amazing variety of some of the world's most awe-inspiring scenery. Much of it has been preserved in national sites—parks, monuments and recreation areas.

Most spectacular of them is Bryce Canyon National Park. Here twelve natural amphitheaters plunge down a thousand feet through the brilliantly multicolored layers of rock. Zion National Park contains some of the most colorful deep narrow canyons, sheer rock walls and unique formations in the plateau country.

Canyonlands National Park features Cataract Canyon, where the Green and Colorado rivers meet. Eroded arches, needles, spires and standing rocks are among the almost unbelievable formations. Capitol Reef National Park contains massive gorges, scarps and Indian artifacts. Some of the formations are white-capped domes like that of the national capitol for which it is named.

The four national monuments are extremely varied. Cedar Breaks is a natural multicolored amphitheater. At Dinosaur National Monument visitors can watch as paleontologists patiently chip away stone to expose the fossilized bones. Hovenweep National Monument features six groups of ancient ruins. Rainbow Bridge National Monument and Natural Bridges National Monument provide the most extensive collection of natural bridges anywhere. Rainbow Bridge itself is often ranked with the "seven natural wonders of the world." Quite different is Tampanogos Cave National Monument, made up of three separate underground wonders.

Golden Spike National Historical Site marks the historic completion of the first railroad across the continent.

Almost every city in Utah adds its story to the success of the Mormons in building civilization in the wilderness. Logan is particularly attractive during the Festival of the American West. Almost all of Beaver has historic interest, and St. George features Brigham Young's winter quarters. The Mormon temple and tabernacle at St. George are architectural standouts. Brigham City is also noted for its tabernacle. Provo boasts of the largest Fourth of July celebration in America, Provo Freedom Festival. Brigham Young University there is said to be the nation's largest private institution of its kind.

Salt Lake City, of course, is the pulsing heart of Utah. It is sometimes labeled "the most beautifully situated city in the world." Visitors to the city generally begin at Temple Square, a one-of-a-kind place, the heart of the worldwide Mormon church. The spires of the imposing temple, the organ and choir of the spacious Tabernacle and the soaring Seagull Monument are only a small part of the square's attractions.

Salt Palace Center encompasses five blocks of buildings devoted to an arena and exhibit hall, art center, symphony hall and Capitol Theatre.

The imposing capitol on Capitol Hill provides a fine view of the city and most of the great valley. It is a good example of Corinthian style architecture. The University of Utah offers many attractions.

The unique quality of Great Salt Lake and its many attractions must be seen to be believed.

To the east are all the attractions of the mountains, including some of the world's most noted ski resorts, which Utahans call "the greatest snow on earth."

No short account could begin to mention all the attractions of Utah, which certainly is "a land unto itself."

COMPAC-FACS
UTAH
Beehive State

HISTORY
Statehood: January 4, 1896
Admitted as: 45th state
Capital: Salt Lake City, founded 1847

The massive capitol was completed in record time. Its huge murals and 3-ton chandelier are prominent features

OFFICIAL SYMBOLS
Motto: Industry
Symbol: Beehive
Animal: Rocky Mountain elk
Bird: Seagull
Fish: Rainbow trout
Flower: Sego lily
Tree: Blue spruce
Song: "Utah, We Love Thee"
GEO-FACS
Area: 84,899 sq. mi.
Rank in Area: 11th
Length (n/s): 345 mi.
Width (e/w): 275 mi.
Geographic Center: In Sanpete Co., 3 mi. n of Manti
Highest Point: 13,528 ft. (Kings Peak)
Lowest Point: 2,000 ft. (Beaverdam Creek)
Mean Elevation: 6,100 ft.
Temperature, Extreme Range: 185 degrees
Number of Counties: 29

POPULATION
Total: 1,652,000 (1984)
Rank: 35th
Density: 20.1 persons per sq. mi.
Principal Cities: Salt Lake City, 163,697; Provo, 74,108; Ogden, 64,407; Orem, 52,399; Sandy City, 52,210; Bountiful, 32,877; West Jordan, 27,192; Logan, 26,844; Murray, 25,750
EDUCATION
Schools: 362 elementary and secondary
Higher: 14
VITAL STATISTICS
Births (1980/83): 135,000
Deaths (1980/83): 27,000
Hospitals: 42
Drinking Age: 21
INTERESTING PEOPLE
Brigham Young, Loretta Young, Zane Gray, Phyllis McGinley, Bernard De Voto, Mahonri Young, John Wesley Powell, Philo T. Farnsworth, John M. Brown, Jonathan Browning, Harvey Fletcher, John Henry Seely, Chief Kanosh, Chief Washakie, Jacob Hamblin, George E. Dern, Ivy Baker Priest, Ezra Taft Benson, the Osmond family, George Romney, Maude Adams
WHEN DID IT HAPPEN?
1776: Exploration of Dominiquez and Escalante
1819: Fur trappers first arrive
1824: Bridger reaches Great Salt Lake
1825: Initial trapper rendezvous on Green River, Henry's Fork
1826: Jedediah Smith crosses
1843: Fremont commences exploration
1844: Fort Buenaventura begun
1847: Mormon pioneers, Salt Lake City founded
1848: Crops saved by gulls
1849: 49'ers arrive
1850: Utah Territory
1861: Telegraph connects the outside world
1869: Utah site of continental railroad completion
1877: Death of Brigham Young
1882: Anti-polygamy law passes Congress
1890: Polygamy abandoned
1896: Statehood
1909: Discovery of Rainbow Bridge
1914: 20,000 in World War I
1941: World War II service for 70,000
1947: Centennial celebrated
1962: Flaming Gorge Dam topped out
1983: Disastrous floods
1985: Copper mining ceases

WYOMING

FASCINATING WYOMING

Wyoming is a state with a split personality. It keeps up-to-date with the latest in technology, but its heart is still in the Old West. Reminders of that past have been lovingly preserved around the state, and each year the state celebrates for nine days with the rip-roaringest recreation of western events staged anywhere.

Wyoming has lived up to its nickname as The Equality State, with the country's first vote for women, the first woman politician, the first woman governor and the greatest plainswoman of the west. Nor will the Indians ever forget the strong pale women for whom they gave the feast of the fattest dogs.

The state is a land of many scenic "firsts," a land of the split divide, the 13,000-foot-high block of stone, the devilish landscape, the most hot water and the lake that roars.

Before modern time began, there was a 245-foot wheel and a mysterious stone cross. In early historic days feathers were given as medals of honor; they may have been won with glass arrowheads. Also notable were the pioneer business conventions held in tents.

Nor can anyone forget the buffalo and their telephone poles.

In modern times travelers on the "nation's mainstreet" marvel at the three-ton head.

Recently, Wyoming became completely up-to-date with close encounters of the third kind.

THE FACE OF WYOMING

Wyoming can boast of a number of geographic distinctions.

One of the most unusual is the fact that Wyoming is the only state made up of parts of all four of the major territories added to the U.S. west of the Mississippi—Louisiana Purchase, Oregon Territory, Texas annexation and territory gained through the War with Mexico.

Another unique feature is the splitting of the Continental Divide. This split forms the Great Divide Basin. Waters falling in this basin do not flow to any ocean but remain trapped in the basin. The divide has other remarkable features. South of Yellowstone Park is Two Ocean Pass. At high water two creeks are joined, but one sends its flow to the Atlantic, the other to the Pacific. In still another feature of the divide, Isa Lake in Yellowstone Park has outlets to both oceans.

Wyoming is one of three states with borders that are entirely manmade and one of two that on a map appear to be perfect rectangles. Montana occupies all of the northern border and a small part of the border on the west. Utah, Colorado, Nebraska and South Dakota are the other neighboring states.

Wyoming is generally considered a plateau, but its surface is broken by a number of mountain ranges. However, the only major opening in the Rocky Mountain chain lies across all of southern Wyoming. This provided the one generally level route from one side of the great range to the other.

Many travel experts call the Teton Range, topped by the Grand Teton and Mt. Moran, the most beautiful and

spectacular in America. Much of this spectacular quality is due to the abrupt rise of the Tetons from the deep valley known as Jackson Hole. The state's most extensive mountain group is the Wind River Range in the northwest. After the break in the Rockies, the range resumes with the Medicine Bow Mountains and Park Range on the Colorado border.

Much of the beauty of the Tetons is due to their lovely lakes. Jackson Lake with its mountain reflections is one of the most photographed scenes anywhere. Jenny Lake is a mountain gem. Yellowstone Lake, in Yellowstone Park, is the highest large lake in the country.

Flaming Gorge Reservoir is the largest of the state's manmade lakes, and many others dot the state.

Rivers of the state send their waters to three major river systems—the Colorado, emptying into the Gulf of California; the Snake-Columbia, emptying into the Pacific; and the Missouri-Mississippi, flowing into the Gulf of Mexico.

Three mighty rivers begin in Wyoming: the Snake, the Yellowstone and the Green. The Bear River crosses Wyoming boundaries at two different places in the small section of the state lying in the Great Basin.

The hot springs at Thermopolis are considered to be the largest mineral hot springs in the world.

Great canyons have been carved into the face of Wyoming by the rivers. The Grand Canyon of the Snake begins at Alpine Junction. One of nature's best-known works is the Grand Canyon of the Yellowstone River in Yellowstone Park. Tensleep Canyon, Rainbow Canyon of

Opposite, Cheyenne

the Badlands, Flaming Gorge and Shell Canyon are other remarkable clefts.

Satan and his territory have given names to several of the truly remarkable features that dot the Wyoming countryside. Devils Tower is perhaps the most striking example of any formation of its type; it was formed by columns of molton rock pushing through the soil as if squeezed from a huge toothpaste tube. Devil's Gate and Hell's Half Acre are other formations with "devilish" names.

The slender stemmed toadstools and red spires of Castle Gardens, Independence Rock and mysterious stretches of Church Butte are all notable landmarks of the state.

Although the great glaciers never reached Wyoming, they chilled the climate so that large mountain glaciers were formed. When they melted, the water enlarged many of the lakes far beyond their present size. Yellowstone Lake was so deep that it emptied into the Pacific instead of the Atlantic.

One of the greatest prehistoric forces operating to form Wyoming was the Teton Uplift. The Tetons were shoved up out of the earth in a single giant block of stone, called block fault mountains.

Even earlier in prehistoric times, much of the Wyoming area was covered by ancient seas, which came and went as the land rose and fell during past eons.

Among the many notable discoveries of prehistoric plants and animals was the renowned horned dinosaur found at Lance Creek. The Como Bluff dinosaur field has yielded discoveries since 1877. Fossil fish are particularly interesting. Wyoming even has a town of Fossil, named for the neighboring cliffs.

The petrified forest near Medicine

The Tetons

Bow also has yielded notable discoveries.

Of course, the greatest fascination of Wyoming is found in the vast area of Yellowstone National Park. Here the fierce underground forces break through the surface, sending lofty plumes of hot water and steam, creating lovely hot pools of the most beautiful vivid colors; here the Yellowstone River sends its two major waterfalls into one of the most vivid canyons, carved into the most fantastic shapes.

Wyoming has a dry climate with wide extremes of temperature. However, the dry air makes the extremes less difficult to endure. Winter blizzards can be severe, driven by winds as high as 80 miles an hour. Winter can change to near summer almost instantly when a heated Chinook wind blows in.

Visitors are cautioned to avoid the dry stream beds during rains, as they sometimes become raging torrents of water, sweeping away everything in their path.

EARLY DWELLERS

A 245-foot wheel, a 58-foot arrow with a 5-foot arrowhead, an ancient

---

THAT'S CURIOUS:

The Indians called Bull Lake "the lake that roars." The sound actually comes from wind lifting the ice and then letting it down with a roar. Indian legend, however, said the sound was the call of a rare white buffalo which drowned in the lake while being hunted for his unique skin.

granite structure near the top of Grand Teton—these are all mysteries of Wyoming's prehistoric past.

The great wheel was formed by some prehistoric group in an unknown past. The rim is made up of large stones, with an even larger stone in the center; 28 spokes reach out from the center to the rim; spaced around the rim are six primitive stone huts.

The great wheel is a complete mystery. It was equally mysterious to the Indians of a later time, but they thought it was connected with religious worship, perhaps with "good medicine," so it became known as the Medicine Wheel.

The tools, weapons and utensils found in Wyoming are all from the Stone Age, with no metallic work being uncovered in the area.

Prehistoric wall paintings and carvings are among the most interesting anywhere, including some of the rare red-painted kind. Others have been placed high upon cliff walls on seemingly impossible places.

Early explorers discovered stone quarries and thought they had been worked by Europeans, so they were called the Spanish Diggings. Although this is now thought unlikely, such quarried items there as a stone cross are not easy to explain.

Between the time of the prehistoric peoples and early European exploration, present Wyoming had few permanent dwellers. At that time the Crows were the first known group in the region, and they were being pushed out by Shoshone, Sioux, Flathead, Arikara, Arapaho, Cheyenne, Blackfoot Ute, Kiowo, Modoc and Gros Ventre.

An extremely primitive group, known as Sheepeater, lived in the Yellowstone area, which was shunned by other tribes. It is thought that most of the Indians considered the region to be haunted because of its geysers and other features.

The Wyoming Indians made distinctive tepees by which they could be identified. Their magnificent war bonnets were symbols of their distinction in battle, each feather standing for a separate battle honor.

Young Indians proved they deserved to be called "braves" by stealing a horse or by taking an enemy scalp.

The volcanic glass called obsidian was used to make arrowheads. Body paint was used in frightening colors and designs. Some groups traveled over the 15-foot deep snows on well-made snowshoes. When the Indians traveled, they kept track of the distance by the number of times they slept at night. Because a certain place was just ten sleeps away from Yellowstone as well as Fort Laramie, it became known by its present name—Tensleep.

The Sioux had migrated to the region from the east, but they grew so fond of the land they considered it sacred.

Two animals were of the utmost importance—the horse and the buffalo. The plains Indians were noted for their horsemanship and for their skill in killing buffalo, which provided food, shelter and clothing.

THAT'S CURIOUS:

Experts feel that the Medicine Wheel is similar in many ways to the better-known prehistoric remains of Stonehenge in England as well as one in the Gobi Desert. However, no one can understand how these three could be connected in any way.

By 1792 the Jesuits had mapped the Bighorn Mountains, and this data must have been picked up at an even earlier time. However, where John Colter entered present Wyoming in 1807, scouting for the trader Manuel Lisa, he was the first white man of record in the region. His greatest fame came when he discovered the wonders of Yellowstone. In a great loop around the area he also discovered the Tetons and Teton Pass.

When Colter returned to civilization, people refused to believe his story of the thermal wonders he had seen in Yellowstone. They called it Colter's Hell.

In 1811 Wilson Price Hunt's party was the first known to have crossed the present state. Returning from Oregon, Robert Stuart's party did pioneer work in blazing the Oregon Trail, even though in reverse of the general direction.

General William H. Ashley installed a trading center on the Yellowstone River outside present Wyoming. He started a series of meetings known as the annual Rendezvous. They brought together trappers, traders, Indians and others who wanted to do business in furs and supplies. These meetings were among the most colorful business gatherings ever held.

The first Rendezvous was held on the Green River, and these meetings continued until 1840—"brawling, colorful events" where fortunes were made and lost; games, contests and fights added to the bustle of as many as 1,500 Indian men, women, children and dogs mingling with the white mountain men.

The major expedition of Captain B.L.E. de Bonneville deepened the tracks of the Oregon Trail in 1832. Dr. Marcus Whitman and the Reverend Samuel Parker visited the 1836 Rendezvous with their wives.

EARLY GROWTH

Fort Laramie had been established in 1834, the first permanent settlement in present Wyoming.

Frontiersman Jim Bridger established Fort Bridger in 1842. With the passage of the thousands of Mormons beginning in 1846 and the eager gold seekers of 1849, an incredible total of more than 100,000 people had passed through an area which had been only a wilderness a few years before. During the days of the pioneer immigrants, 34,000 are said to have died.

In 1853 Mormons established Fort Supply and Deer Creek, the first farming settlements in the present state.

In a great powwow at Laramie, the Indians had signed a peace agreement. That peace was broken in 1854, and Indian battles continued for about 35 years. The year 1865 was known as "the bloody year on the plains." Settlers, wagon trains and stagecoach stations were attacked. Chief Red Cloud massacred an army group under W.J. Fetterman, and besieged Fort Kearny with 2,500 warriors.

John "Portugee" Phillips made a desperate 237-mile ride through terrible weather to Fort Laramie and returned to Kearny with help, and the siege was broken.

In 1867 Chief Red Cloud lost over a thousand of his men in a battle with Captain James Powell, and he never regained his power.

UP-TO-DATE

By 1867 the first intercontinental railroad was moving across Wyoming.

New settlements sprang up along the right of way, including Cheyenne. Building the railroad was one of the great epics of mankind. The building crews were harrassed over almost every mile by Indian attack, storms, snows and lack of supplies, but they kept on, and finally in 1869 Wyoming lay almost in the middle of tracks stretching from coast to coast. Major cities of the east and west were now days away instead of weeks.

By July 25 of that year, Congress created Wyoming Territory, but it was not organized until the next year, with Cheyenne as the capital.

Wyoming had not yet become a state when in 1869 it became the first American government to grant the vote to women.

The first scientific expedition to visit Yellowstone described their great amazement at the giant column of water and steam that shot into the air from one of the geysers. Finding that it erupted regularly, they named it Old Faithful.

At the urging of one member of the expedition, Cornelius Hedges, Congress set aside for all time the wonders of the area as the first National Park. The first preserve of its kind in the world, Yellowstone National Park came into being March 1, 1872.

One of the great episodes of Wyoming history was the movement of cattle from Texas to the grazing lands of the area. By 1884 over 800,000 cattle had been herded up over the Long Trail or the Texas Trail. By that time the Cattle Kings ruled the state. At one time 120,000 head of cattle roamed the vast Two Bar Cattle Company holdings, which was one of many gigantic ranch corporations.

The terrible winter of 1886 killed thousands of cattle; homesteaders began to claim land and fence in parts of the range. Feuds between the cattle ranchers and farmers (Nesters) were frequent. One of the most violent was known as the Johnson County Cattle War in 1892. It might have become a real and serious shooting war if the army had not arrived at the last moment.

By this time the "Wild West" days of Wyoming were about over. The thefts of rustlers, the work of vigilante committees, the hanging of outlaws had provided background for innumerable movie and television scripts, but law and order finally came about.

In 1890 Wyoming did not have the necessary population; nevertheless, Congress approved statehood on July 10 of that year.

The early 1900's involved the ranchers in new quarrels, this time with the sheep ranchers. Cattlemen were known to disguise themselves with gunnysacks over their heads before going out to shoot sheep.

President Theodore Roosevelt came west to visit Yellowstone in 1906. He also declared Devil's Tower to be the first national monument.

Wyoming became part of the first national "mainstreet" when the Lincoln Highway crossed the state in 1913.

A total of seven percent of Wyoming's population saw service in World War I.

THAT'S CURIOUS:

The Indians were amazed that the first white women they had ever seen could appear so pale and yet were strong enough to make such a journey. The Indians provided a great feast in honor of the first white women in Wyoming, serving the fattest dogs available.

PEOPLES

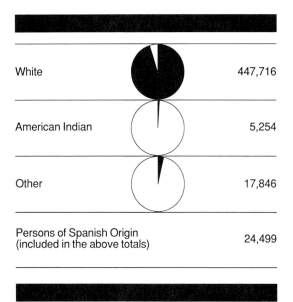

White		447,716
American Indian		5,254
Other		17,846
Persons of Spanish Origin (included in the above totals)		24,499

The state had the best record of all for percentage of draftees who qualified for service in that war.

The scandal of bribery and other charges stemming from the lease of Wyoming's Teapot Dome oil fields in 1923-24 was one of the worst of its kind in the federal government, but Wyoming officials were not involved, and Wyoming Senator John B. Kendrick was one of the main investigators of the affair.

Also in 1924, Wyoming was one of the first two states ever to elect a woman governor—Nellie Tayloe Ross.

In 1940 the state celebrated 30 years of statehood. Jackson Hole became a national monument in 1950, and Fort Laramie was named a national historic site in 1960. When Wyoming celebrated its 75th anniversary of statehood in 1965, it was noted that "the whole history of statehood could easily have passed during

one lifetime," from conestoga wagon to supersonic plane.

In 1980 and 1984 Ronald Reagan won the Wyoming vote for president, but the Democrats continued to hold the governor's chair.

In 1985 and 1986 anthropologist Philip Gingerich discovered human teeth and jawbones near the Yellowstone River. They may prove to be the remains of the first true primate and distantly related to human beings.

PERSONALITIES

Sixty years of rule would be a good record for any monarch. Wyoming's great Washakie, chief of the Shoshone, controlled his people benevolently but firmly for that long period.

As a diplomat, he might have served in any embassy. He never took his people to war with the European invaders but worked in a way that brought the Washakie benefits not won by other tribes. The chief "understood the history of his time better than many statesmen," according to one observer.

Part of his success was due to the fact that more than other Indian leaders, he understood that the white people would continue to be stronger and more numerous and that they had the strength of a powerful government behind them. He realized that in the end the Indians would never win.

His son-in-law, Crazy Horse, would never agree with the older man's belief, and along with Chief Red Cloud, he was one of the most violent in opposition to the white flood of immigrants and settlers.

Washakie finally agreed to settlement on the reservation. He is believed to have lived to more than 100 years of age before his death in 1909.

The name of Washakie is remembered in many Wyoming localities, including Fort Washakie where he is buried.

From the beginning of its formal government, Wyoming has lived up to its name as the Equality State. Esther Hobert Morris was one of those most responsible for this. She became the first woman to serve in a judicial post, as Justice of the Peace at South Pass. She was a leader in movements to promote the vote for women.

Nellie Tayloe Ross served not only as one of the first two women governors but also was appointed by F.D. Roosevelt to be the director of the Mint.

Martha Canary's ability as a scout on the plains was said to equal any man's. She guided many a party across the wilderness including many government troops. She told a story about one such occasion. "Captain Egan was in command...returning to the post we were ambushed...Captain Egan was shot. I...saw the captain reeling in his saddle as though about to fall. I turned my horse and galloped back...and got there in time to catch him as he was falling. I lifted him onto my horse in front of me and succeeded in getting him safely to the post. Captain, on recovering, laughingly said, 'I name you Calamity Jane, the heroine of the plains.'"

The name Calamity Jane is still remembered; she stood as one of the symbols of the old west.

Another of the great guides was Jim Bridger. A friend said of him, "...others failed to reach the high standard of efficiency which so characterized his work as a scout...his ability to map out any part of the territory entirely from memory was uncanny."

Another notable pioneer in the region was John Colter. He had been with Lewis and Clark, then left them to stay in the Wyoming country. Colter is best known for his discovery of the wonders of Yellowstone. However, he also discovered the source of the Snake River and the Tetons and Jackson Hole. He was the first explorer of the Bighorn and Wind rivers.

Buffalo Bill Cody spent much of his later life in Wyoming, where he founded the town of Cody and guided many hunting parties. Among many other accomplishments, he made the longest Pony Express ride on record, keeping on for a total of 322 miles after his replacement had been killed.

Prominent novelists Owen Wister and Emerson Hough wrote of the life of the area. Thomas Moran did much of his painting in Wyoming. His "Grand Canyon of the Yellowstone" is one of the best-known works in the national capitol. Mount Moran in the Tetons carries his name.

One of America's merchandising giants was J.C. Penney, who started his first store at Kemmerer.

Early cowboy movie star Tim McCoy also held a government post in Wyoming.

A WEALTH OF NATURE

"On nearly every rim a small furry reddish-buff beast sat on his hind legs...as we passed gave a warning yelp, shook his tail, and with a ludicrous flourish of its hind legs dived into its hole." English

THE ECONOMY

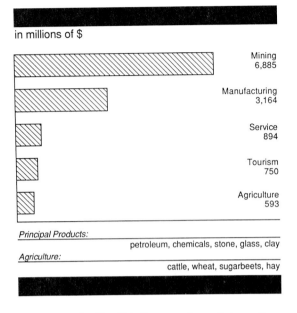

in millions of $

Mining	6,885
Manufacturing	3,164
Service	894
Tourism	750
Agriculture	593

Principal Products:
petroleum, chemicals, stone, glass, clay

Agriculture:
cattle, wheat, sugarbeets, hay

writer Isabella Bird was describing the prairie dog. The millions of the little animals have disappeared, and only a few remain.

The once innumerable buffalo have also gone except for protected herds.

Yellowstone is one of the world's great animal sanctuaries, and the world's largest herd of elk still flourishes at Jackson Hole.

The bald eagle, wild turkey and trumpeter swan may still be seen. An unusual bird, the water ouzel, nests behind waterfalls and hunts food along the bottom of streams.

Far from being barren, the prairies and mountains of the state have hosted more than 2,500 varieties of seed-bearing plants, and billions of feet of lumber could be harvested from the forest land.

Vast reserves of coal and the sixth largest petroleum reserves in the nation form part of the enormous mineral storehouse of Wyoming, much still untapped.

Although a seemingly dry state, Wyoming has abundant water, including large reserves of groundwater.

USING THE WEALTH

Mineral production is far and away the leading industry of Wyoming. It ranks sixth among all the states in value of mineral produced. In the short space of 20 years, the state's modest coal production grew until it ranks as the leading coal producer of the west. The state ranks first in production of bentonite and soda ash and second in uranium.

Wyoming still holds sixth rank among all the petroleum-producing states. This is a far cry from pioneer times when oil seeped up from the ground, and Indians sold it to the wagon trains to lubricate the wheels.

Cattle ranks first in Wyoming agricultural income. The state ranks third in number of sheep produced. Wheat, sugar beets and hay are the leading crops.

Manufacturing is mostly concerned with processing the local mineral and agricultural products.

Transportation boasts some of its

THAT'S CURIOUS:

When telegraph poles were first put up across Wyoming, the buffalo discovered they made perfect scratching posts. They pushed so hard that sometimes the posts were uprooted. When the linesmen lined the posts with sharp spikes, they were even more attractive, and there were reports of 20 or 30 buffalo waiting in turn to get to the posts.

120

most picturesque phases in Wyoming, including the short-lived Pony Express.

GETTING AROUND

Nothing like Yellowstone Park exists anywhere else—with its combination of 10,000 thermal features, including famous Old Faithful geyser along with awesome scenery. Geysers are formed when cold water filters down into the rocks to reach the superheated rocks far below. Through a tube formed in the rock, steaming columns of water shoot into the air spectacularly. Giant Geyser reaches a height of 250 feet, the record for the park. Thermal conditions are constantly changing. Most severe changes followed the earthquake of 1959, bringing extensive alterations. Among many others, Sapphire Pool suddenly started erupting like a geyser.

The beautiful steaming pools that dot the landscape are lined with brilliantly colored algae. Because each variety thrives in a different temperature of water, the colors vary with the temperature of the water, so there are dozens of the brightest colors. Grand Prismatic Spring is one of the most striking of this type. It takes its name from the variety of colors, all reflected in the clouds of steam above.

Mammoth Hot Springs has been built up over the years by limestone brought to the surface by the hot water. This limestone has formed lofty terraces of the most fantastic colors and shapes.

Even without its thermal wonders, Yellowstone would be one of the world's leading attractions because of its natural beauty. Visitors standing at the rim of the Grand Canyon of the Yellowstone River exclaim at the world of eroded rock shapes in varying shades of yellow, and, of course, at the end of the canyon, the world-famed scene of beautiful lower Falls of the Yellowstone. Upriver is another falls, Upper Falls, overshadowed by Lower Falls but still of great beauty.

Huge Yellowstone Lake with its fishing, Obsidian Cliff, the hiking and in the winter the snowmobiling, all combine with the winsome bears and other wildlife to make the region one of the world's great natural marvels.

Not content with one marvel, Wyoming provides another only a short distance south of Yellowstone. Whether or not the Teton Mountains can be called the "most beautiful anywhere," they certainly must be ranked among the very top. Mirrored in the lakes at their feet, the peaks of Teton National Park offer unparalleled scenery.

But scenery is far from all. The Jackson Hole region is noted for skiing. Float trips down the Snake River, horseback riding and mountain climbing are other attractions.

Northern Wyoming offers much else for the visitor to see and do. Far to the east is another national site. Devils Tower National Monument lifts its fantastically wrinkled shaft out of a valley, to stand majestically alone. Movie fans got tempting glimpses of the area in "Close Encounters of the Third Kind."

The nearby town of Sundance has also been featured in movies.

Bighorn Canyon National Recreation Area near Lovell provides a wild scenic beauty. Over the mountain and slightly south, Thermopolis Hot Springs State Park features the world's largest mineral hot springs. Buffalo Bill's home town,

The ghost towns have their own attractions

Cody, is noted for its Buffalo Bill Museum, the Whitney Gallery of Western Art, the Plains Indian Museum and the Winchester Museum.

From Cody, the gateway to Yellowstone winds breathtakingly through the Wapiti Valley and has been called the most scenic 50 miles in the world, as it passes through Shoshone National Forest—the nation's first.

What historic memories the visitor will find crossing central Wyoming on the Oregon Trail, the First Road West—historic sites, wagon ruts, military establishments, trading posts and Pony Express stations are all memories of that pioneer time.

Fort Laramie National Historic Site preserves the structures that reflect the drama of this outpost of the west, including Suttlers Store, the oldest build-

ing remaining in Wyoming. Near Casper, the state's largest city, Fort Casper and the Casper Mountain recreation areas, Independence Rock, Hell's Half Acre and the Wind River Indian Reservation may all be visited.

Interstate 80 across Wyoming follows the route laid out by the pathfinders and followed by the first transcontinental railroad. The sparkling gold-leaf dome of the capitol looms up from any approach to Cheyenne. Each year, the capital city hosts one of the nation's premiere celebrations—Cheyenne Frontier Days. Some experts consider the Frontier Days rodeo the finest anywhere. The nine-day celebration also includes four parades, Indian dancing and much other entertainment. Frontier Days Old West Museum at Cheyenne features memorabilia from the first rodeo in 1897 to the present, including some of the most interesting horse-drawn vehicles and Indian costumes.

Jacques La Ramie gave Laramie its name, and the city is now one of the cultural centers of the high country, mostly centered in the highly rated University of Wyoming. At the top of Sherman Hill is one of the unusual and unexpected attractions of the area, the 3.5 ton bronze head of Lincoln by University of Wyoming sculptor Robert Russin.

Laramie is the center for a fine mountain resort area in the Snowy Range. In summer visitors may travel over the mountains on state route 130.

The so-called Red Desert is one of the world's truly unique areas, the Great Divide Basin—a "hole" in the Continental Divide which drains only into itself.

East of Eden is a region of sand dunes stretching for more than 100 miles. The dunes take on fantastic form and offer recreation such as the thrilling dune wagon rides.

Flaming Gorge National Recreation Area surrounds Flaming Gorge Lake. Firehole Canyon north of Black's Fork is especially spectacular with its chimneys and pinnacles reflecting in the blue water of the lake. The lake is renowned for its fishing and boating.

Fort Bridger, built in 1842 by Jim Bridger and partner Louis Vasquez, has long been in the process of restoration.

The old fort is a timely reminder of the hardships and sacrifices experienced along this route during some of the most picturesque periods of American history. Wyoming keeps full pace with modern technology, but its heart still belongs to the Old West.

COMPAC-FACS

WYOMING
Equality State—Cowboy State

HISTORY
Statehood: July 10, 1890
Admitted as: 44th state
Capital: Cheyenne, founded 1867
OFFICIAL SYMBOLS
Motto: Equal rights
Bird: Meadowlark (sturnella neglecta)
Flower: Indian paintbrush (castilleja linariaefolia)
Tree: Plains cottonwood (populus sargentii)
Gem: Jade (nephrite)
Insignia (unofficial): Bucking Horse, designed by Allan True
Song: "Wyoming"
GEO-FACS
Area: 97,809 sq. mi.
Rank in Area: 9th
Length (n/s): 275 mi.
Width (e/w): 365 mi.
Geographic Center: In Fremont Co., 58 mi. ene of Lander
Highest Point: 13,804 ft. (Gannett Peak)
Lowest Point: 3,100 ft. (Belle Fourche River)
Mean Elevation: 6,700 ft.
Temperature, Extreme Range: 177 degrees
Number of Counties: 23 (plus Yellowstone National Park)
POPULATION
Total: 511,000 (1984)
Rank: 49th
Density: 5.3 persons per sq. mi.
Principal Cities: Casper, 51,016; Cheyenne, 47,283; Laramie, 24,410; Rock Springs, 19,458; Sheridan, 15,146; Green River, 12,807; Gillette, 12,134
EDUCATION
Schools: 371 elementary and secondary
Higher: 8
VITAL STATISTICS
Births (1980/83): 35,000
Deaths (1980/83): 10,000
Hospitals: 31
Drinking Age: 19
INTERESTING PEOPLE
Chief Washakie, Crazy Horse, Red Cloud, Esther Hobart Morris, Nellie Tayloe Ross, Martha Canary

123

The capitol

(Calamity Jane), Jim Bridger, John Colter, William H. (Buffalo Bill) Cody, Owen Wister, Emerson Hough, Thomas Moran, J.C. Penney, Tim McCoy

WHEN DID IT HAPPEN?

1807: John Colter explores
1811: Wyoming crossed by Hunt expedition
1812: Stuart party crosses
1824: First traders' Rendezvous
1834: Fort Laramie founded, first permanent settlement
1842: First Fremont expedition
1843: Fort Bridger becomes 2nd settlement
1847: Mormon migration
1849: Rush of the 49'ers
1860: Short life of the Pony Express
1861: Telegraph edges out Pony Express
1866: Fetterman massacre
1867: Founding of Cheyenne
1869: Continental railroad completed; Wyoming
1872: Territory established, Yellowstone National Park established, first such preserve in world

1887: Terrible winter destroys cattle, bankrupts stockmen
1890: Statehood
1892: Johnson County Cattle War
1897: Frontier Days first celebrated at Cheyenne
1902: Wyoming is site of first national forest
1906: First national monument, Devils Tower
1924: Nellie Tayloe Ross becomes one of two first women governors
1929: Establishment of Grand Teton National Park
1938: Fort Laramie declared a national monument
1940: 50th birthday of statehood celebrated
1950: Jackson Hole National Monument established
1959: Earthquake shakes, alters Yellowstone
1965: Statehood Diamond Jubilee
1976: Carter receives state vote
1980: Reagan popular state choice
1985: Human jawbone discovered; may be missing link

INDEX to this volume

ACKNOWLEDGMENTS

Maps, charts and graphs, EBE; Santa Fe Southern Pacific Corp., 2, 8, 11, 17, 24, 30, 86, 88, 94; Stuart Collection, EBE;, 6, 12, 59; USGS/NHAP/EROS, 14, 28, 42, 56, 70, 84, 99, 112; Arizona Office of Tourism, 23, 26 EBE;, 32, 38; Denver Metropolitan Convention and Tourist Bureau, 40; R. Laurent, 45; USDI, NPS, Nez Perce Nat. Hist. Park, 50; Idaho Travel Council, Div. of Dept. of Commerce, 52, 54; Montana Travel Promotion Unit, 67, 68; Woolaroc Museum, 63; "Nevada Magazine," 72, 82; Nevada Dept. of Economic Development, 78; C. R. Laurent, 80, 114; New Mexico Tourism and Travel Div., 96; Utah Travel Council, 100, 103; Salt Lake Valley Convention and Visitors Bureau, 110; Wyoming Travel Commission, 122, 124